The Breakthrough

ARKEMI "KIM" ROBINSON

authorHOUSE®

AuthorHouse™
1663 Liberty Drive, Suite 200
Bloomington, IN 47403
www.authorhouse.com
Phone: 1-800-839-8640

First published by AuthorHouse 05/05/2009

ISBN: 978-1-4389-6415-7 (sc)

Printed in the United States of America
Bloomington, Indiana

This book is printed on acid-free paper.

About the Author

Arkemi "Kim" Wakeetta Robinson is a native of New Orleans, Louisiana. She currently lives in her home town of New Orleans and is the mother of two wonderful sons, Mikeze' and Dante' Shipp. Although "The Breakthrough" is Arkemi's first book, she will be writing more! The characters in this book were inspired and created by those life situations that she knows most of her readers have experienced. Those of you who have, or are still dealing with situations similar to those displayed in "The Breakthrough." Arkemi wants you to keep your head up and pray. Learn to let go and let God handle it. Thank you again for supporting this book and be on the look out for her next books "Preparing To Be His Wife" and "The Streets Is Not Where I Wanna Be." May God Bless you all.

Acknowledgements

First and foremost, I want to thank
God the head of my life.
I want to thank my parents. Aundra and Edward
Smith who always had a listening ear anytime I
discussed my book. I love ya'll. My sister's and
brother's, Latrina Robinson Tshiteya, Leon (Al)
Harris, Raymond Smith boy your heart goes a
mile a second. I appreciate you giving me a helping
hand. Dianca Smith and Charles Smith smoochies.
Ant Cynthia you are amazing. My sister in law
and brother in law and all the rest of ya'll. To my
nieces and nephews Tee Kim love ya'll. To my
wonderful children Mikeze' Danny Shipp and Dante'
Michael Shipp, Momma loves ya'll dearly. Thank
you for ya'll patience when momma would close
her bedroom door and write for long hours. Words
can't even describe how much I appreciate ya'll. To
my wonderful godmother Wendolyn Logan I love
sooooo much thanks for everything you do for me.
To my cousins Leslie, Elmetta (Bunny) Johnson,
and Angela, who inspired me to write this book.
Bunny thanks for staying up all those late nights
with me fussing, smiling, and saying I can't wait
till we finish this one so we can start on the next
one. I really appreciate it. Bishop Paul and Pastor
Debra B. Morton. I want to thank ya'll for all the
time ya'll gave me it was and still is appreciated.
To my best friend Toya Bilbo, I love you so much
thank you for putting up with my craziness. Antoine
"Fe" Banks thanks for lending a helping hand we

appreciate it. To my family and friends, thank you for all the support, I love ya'll. Thanks, Brandi for that beautiful CD "Human" I wrote most of my book to that album. Last but not least, Danny Shipp because of you I am now able to face my challenges. Thank you. God bless you all that supported me.

This book is dedicated to all the women and men that are in an unhealthy relationship or that have ever been in an unhealthy relationship. Remember the choice is yours, only you can make the decision to get out. When you read this book you will realize that a lot of us have experienced some of the things that these people experienced if not all woman or man. The relationship becomes unhappy when one knows that they still want to play the field. That eventually destroys the relationship. This book is really interesting not because I wrote it, but because when you read it, you will feel it. You have to read the "The Breakthrough" in order to understand my next book "Preparing to Be His Wife." Also look forward for "The Streets Is Not Where I Wanna Be.

The Breakthrough

By: Arkemi "Kim" Robinson

Have you ever been hurt by a mate you truly loved? Ever wonder why men cheat? Ever wonder why women cheat? Ever thought about how physical and mental abusing relationships affect kids? Do you think low self-esteem takes apart of it? Did you ever stop to think if kids are involve how this takes a toll on them? Who do we fault? Who can help us? There is a scenario for all of this and we are going to get the answer. You know the saying, "If loving you is wrong I don't want to be right." This is what a lot of us say when it comes down to loving our mate. We see it no other way...Dionne told herself that over and over again.

CHAPTER I

One Saturday afternoon while walking through the outlet mall Dionne met a guy. He was tall about six three with caramel colored skin. He had beautiful teeth in his mouth that really attracted Dionne to him. Ron walked up to Dionne and he asks her name in a real cute soft voice. "Hi I'm Dionne, she responded. "D" for short and you are sweetie?" "I'm Ron; I'm out shopping with my boy. If it's possible can I have your number?" "Sure you can have my number but don't take it and not use it." Dionne told Ron. "I will defiantly use it believe that, mumbles Ron. As Dionne was leaving out the mall after a long day of shopping and meeting who she thought was Mr. Right. She calls her friend Lily. "Hello," Lily says when she answered her phone. "Yeah what are you doing?" "Nothing, what you want Dionne? You only call my phone when you bored so you must be bored." "No I'm not bored and then again maybe I am. That's the reason I'm calling you," Dionne tells Lily laughing. "Real funny Dionne." "I just left out the mall and I am so hungry, you trying to go to Outback Steak House?" "Which one?" "The one on the strip. We have a few things we need to talk about." "A few things like what Dionne?" "Your specialty girly, "SEX." "You know who you're having and whom I'm having the birds and bees the stuff that our moms should have thought us when we were young but unfortunately they didn't so we had to learn on our own now doesn't that sound like a deal?" "Yes it does Dionne about what time?" "Let's say about seven or when you send your company home." "For your information noisy I don't have company over here right now…. He just left but seven is good timing see you then crazy." Dionne hangs up the phone debating on which one of her hoochie outfits she would wear on her dinner date with Lily. Maybe I could hook up with Ron once I'm done with dinner with Lily. Dionne thought to herself. Mmm should I wear the fitted pants and jacket the short dress or my shorts with this see through shirt? Which ever set I choose I will be wearing a pair of my six inch heals so I can strut my stuff straight to my next man or somebody else's man. Who knows and who cares. Black Vicki lace booty drawers and bra that will really bring out the sexiness in me. A woman has to feel sexy about herself at all times especially when she don't have a man. Dionne hurried up and took a shower then put her dress on. It was close to seven o'clock the time Dionne was suppose to meet Lily at the restaurant. Dionne was just starting to put her make up on. I know Lily about to be calling me going off on me screaming why you not here yet, and you better hurry up before you are sitting here by yourself. I forgot the title of the subject "SEX" she's not going anywhere.

Lily walks in the restaurant and she looks around. No sign of Dionne. This tramp works on my nerves she's always making plans and always running late. She tells me we can meet at seven and now its seven ten. The hostess walks up. "A table for?" She asks. "Two please ma'am... Lily answers. My slow friend will be here shortly." "Follow me ma'am; I have a booth right here by the window. Is this ok?" "This is fine, thanks." My name is Nikeya and I'll be your server tonight." Dionne finally walks in. "Hey, I'm sorry I'm running late. I was kind of stuck in traffic." "Yeah bitch sure you were. Sit your ass down so we can order I'm damn starving. "May I take your order?" The waitress asks looking at Lily under eye thinking to herself, she's some kind of ghetto." "Steak and baked potato," Dionne sighs. "The same for me," Lily added. While having dinner the girls start their discussion. "Now the best subject in the world besides God is "SEX." "Ok nasty what's up?" Lily screams out. "What is all this talk about SEX?" "Well, I met this guy at the mall today his name is Ron. He is so nice looking. He's tall and girl he is fine as hell. He has pretty teeth and you know how I feel about a man that has nice teeth and he is bo legs with a sexy ass walk that just does something to me. He has a soft voice and smells so good. I wanted to have him right there but you know I'm shy!" Yeah right who she think she's fooling. Lily thought to herself. "He is so attractive if he wouldn't have came up to me I sure would have went up to him telling him, "Boy you're so fine I want you to be mine." "Oh so you want to be a rapper now trying to rhyme and flirt at the same time," Lily says laughing. "Yeah rap right on Ron." "How you even know if that boy want you?" "Are you mad or jealous? I smell it all in the air." "I'm both Dionne." The girls both acknowledged the joke. "So anyway, are you having somebody tonight?" "Having somebody like what Dionne?" "Somebody like who you fucking tonight, you know like the dick enters the pussy type thing." "Since you insist Dionne maybe I'll have Donald tonight all up in me with you not disturbing us ok." "You're kidding right?" "No I'm not." "Whatever girl, the dinner was fantastic," Dionne says. "It was." "Girl lets get going so I can call my new friend and see what he's up to tonight and maybe we can get something going." "Alright girl don't do anything I wouldn't do when you get with Ron." "Don't worry Lily I wont, I'm gone try to be a good girl tonight and control my hormones."

CHAPTER II

Driving home on a breezy winter night, Dionne stopped at a nearby gas station to get a cup of cocoa before going home. It's almost nine thirty, I need to hurry up and get this cocoa so I can try to catch up with Ron to see what he's getting into tonight. If he doesn't have plans maybe we can hook up. When Dionne finally made it home she sits back on her black leather sofa and clicked on her flat screen television to the Kardashians. Oh I need to call Ron.

Ron is at the sports bar chilling with his boys having drinks and shooting pool of course. "Hey boo," Will yells at one of the girls sitting on the bar stool. "Which one of us you're yelling at?" "I want you since you ask," Will replies. Brenda walks over to Will. "What's up? What can I help you with?" A smirk came across Will's face. "If I can tell you what you can help me with tonight of sexy, it would make me happy. "What's that? Brenda asks anxiously wanting to know what Will was trying to get at. "Don't worry about it." "What's your name anyway?" "My bad baby my mind was some other place but my name is Will and yours if I may ask?" "My name is Brenda." "Now back to what I can help you with?" "Well Brenda, I think you look hot tonight. "I try to do my best." "I see you then had you a few drinks. "How you feeling?" "I'm feeling real good right about now. Now get to the point come out with it and just be straight up." "Alright Brenda off the record you think we can hook up and get a room or something if you know what I mean." "Let me take a moment to think about this." "What is it you need to think about?" "Why you want me to come to a hotel room with you, that's what I need to think about." "It will be innocent

I promise." I don't know you like that to be going to no hotel with you." "You coming it's either yes or no." "What are we going to do when we get there?" "Just watch a movie and chill." Will responds sipping his Hennessy. "Ok Will and all we're going to do is watch a movie alright?" "For Sho Brenda that's all we're doing." "Before you leave I'll let you know what's up." "I'll be patiently waiting."

Dionne is at home pacing the floor wondering how it would feel to sleep out with Ron. What would he think of me she thought? I don't even know if he has a girlfriend. That's the question that kept running through Dionne's mind? You know at this moment I really don't care; you know how scandalous women are today and personally I just feel like fucking. I'll call him just to see what he says and if he can't then I have to respect his mind.

"Hey Ron what's up? This Dionne the chick you met at the mall today." "Ok, what's up Dionne what's good?" "Nothing much you ran across my mind so I was just calling to see what's popping? What you up to?" "Chilling at the sports bar having a few drinks and you?" "I was sitting here thinking and I wanted to know if we could hook up, you know just to get to know each other a lil' better." "Cool with me. I need to come get you, you need me to meet you or what?" "No honey, if you don't mind can you come get me." That's not a problem I'll be there round' ten." "Alright I'll be waiting."

CHAPTER III

Tracey screams through the phone to Lily. "Girl you know Ron the one Dionne been dealing with?" "Yeah... What about him?" " Come to find out he has a girlfriend and mess with many more. "Are you serious Tracey?" "Yes, I am so serious and Dina just told me he's a hot boy." Let your friend know but you didn't hear it from me because I don't have time to entertain that you say and I say shit. I guarantee she's fucking him already because if it was me, I would have fucked him by now too!" "What Tracey?" "Sorry but I'm just being real. Real bitches must stay true that's why she's your friend and not mine. I can be in her face laughing and fucking her man, her boo, whatever he is to her and not feel guilty cause that's not my friend ha ha." "I guess Tracy with your scandalous ass." "I know I am don't remind me because I would be tempted but enough of all this call your friend and put her up on game." "I will." "When you moving to Seattle Tracy?" "This Saturday believe me Lily, I will see you before I go. Call me later." "Alright Tracy thanks for the information." "My pleasure."

As soon as Lily hung up with Tracy she was dialing Dionne's number. "Come on, answer your phone Dionne, I have news to give you news about that dog Ron that's so called trying to make you his girl. Ugh! Lily hung up and called right back. Bitch answer the damn phone she bet not be laid up with that no good bastard." "What's up Lily?" "You finally decided to answer the phone. I had to call you ten million times before you answer." "What's going with you sounding like a crazy maniac?" "Are you with Ron?" "Why does it matter to you who I'm with?" "Dionne are you with him or not?" "Yes….I am. "Is he close?" "No he's taking a shower, what's up with all the questions about Ron?" "Well Dionne I just got news he has a girl and a child with her and they live together." "What, Lily are you serious?" "Yes, Tracey knows a friend of the girl and mentioned his name and she remembered me telling her about Ron and she called to tell me so I could put you up on game." "Thanks Lily for looking' out but Ron is only my friend and my sex partner right now. Maybe in the future I'll be worried about if he has a girlfriend or not. I can hear me singing, "I'll take your man." "I'm saying to you Dionne, "Them dogs be creeping" Lily says giggling. "He's coming out the bathroom I'm about to hang up, Dionne whispers. I'll talk to you later." Ron comes out the bathroom with his towel wrapped around him. He sits on the edge of the bed rolling a blunt. "So what's up Dionne?" Ron asks. "Nothing much just enjoying what's in front of me." "Really, so you liking what you see?" "I do," Dionne says as she stands up and takes off her dress. "So what's up with you Ron? Are you in a relationship?" "No, I'm not Ms. Dionne." Ron looks up at Dionne for he is aroused as his eyes focus on Dionne in her Lace booty drawers and no bra. "I do have a female roommate." Ron thought to hisself unable to keep his composure. Seeing Dionne like that made him speechless for a moment. "I do have friends," Ron says coughing from the blunt he was smoking." "That's that fire." Dionne starts dancing in the mirror asking Ron, "Close friends that your intimate with or friends you just conversate with?" "Why is she doing this to me? Damn, my shit rock hard." "I conversate with a few. What about you? Are you in a relationship?" "Nah,

I'm really not ready for no relationship. I only want friends right now but who knows what the future holds, soooo." "I'm twenty-eight Dionne because I know that's your next question." "Well thanks Ron for informing me about that but I don't care about your age. Age is nothing but a number." "No problem then we good." "Yeah, we straight Ronald." Ron sat at the edge of the bed smoking the last piece of his blunt. As he took his last hit he crawled in the bed next to Dionne. "Hey baby," Ron whispered in Dionne's ear while sticking his two fingers inside her. "How does that feel?" "Uh Ron it feels so good baby." Dionne eyes started rolling to the back of her head. "This feels so good." Dionne felt chills go through her entire body. As Ron was pushing his fingers in and out of her Dionne rolled back and forth with him moaning how good it felt to her. Ron now fully aroused inserted himself inside Dionne. As his penis was sliding back and forth inside Dionne, Ron made eye contact with Dionne to acknowledge how wet and good it was to him. "Ugh, spread your legs, so I can go deeper and feel those walls. "Ooo Ron go deeper and deeper. You feel so good inside me, I'm about to have an orgasm. Ron starts going faster and faster inside Dionne that feels so good Dionne mown as she griped Ron's back tight. She pulled him down to suck his neck. This is the best I've ever had," Dionne said as she came to her climax. When they were done Dionne lay next to Ron and he hugged her around the waist and they fell asleep.

CHAPTER IV

Brenda and Will woke up the next morning reminiscing on last night. "Good morning Will," says Brenda as she kisses Will on his jaw. "What's up Brenda? "Nothing much baby." "Man last night was real interesting and I loved every part of it." "Really, Brenda asks Will. Brenda smile ear to ear. "Well I'm glad you had an interesting night, I enjoyed it too. "Well I'm happy I had a chance to please you "B." "That you did! You want me to get us some breakfast?" "Not really, I have to get ready to go; I have some business to take care of."

William Sams is a big business man that owns several houses, two businesses and he drives real nice cars. He owns a Benz, a BMW Coupe and a Bentley. He makes lots of money and a lot of women are interested in dealing with a man like Mr. William Sams.

"You're leaving already we have not eaten breakfast." "Here's a few dollars; go get you something to eat. I have things to do. Just hit me up, call me or text me. I'll see you later." In a hurry Will got his things together so he could leave. Before he could make it completely out the door his phone starts ringing. "What's up?" Will says whispering so Brenda doesn't hear him. "Where you at?" The lady on the other line asks. "I'm leaving from downtown; I was over here by Donald." "I didn't hear from you last night, I thought something was wrong. "I was worried about you." "No, everything's good I was feeling bad last night so I stayed over here by my brother. I'm bout to take care something with my brother. I'll call you back."

Brenda was very upset because of the way Will just up and left her. "I can't believe that no good dog just left me like that. Talking about call me later. I'm gone, I have things to do. They all packaged the same. I'll go eat breakfast by myself on your damn expense. I'll call you on my sweet time sucker. One day I'll learn not to put up with this bullshit from a man."

CHAPTER V

Five years later, Ron and Dionne still kicking it. Dionne found out the truth about what Tracey and Lily told her about Ron being with another girl. It was true all along. He has a son with her. Ron told Dionne she was only his roommate and that they weren't together. The baby momma, Nicollet fought Dionne over Ron. After all that, he still ended up being with Dionne.

"Girl Dionne how have you been since Ron's been gone?" "I'm good, just felling a little stressed raising my daughter out here without Ron." "Have you talked to him yet?" "Yeah I have Ashley." "What he talking about? Is he still playing with his baby momma?" "Well that's one of the reasons he called me to tell me he told her he wanted to be with me." "Girl you think what he's saying is true? "You know how they play games when their looking at those four walls. They think about everything and everybody." "Your right but whatever he says is fine with me." "Enough talk about Ron. Dionne do you have somebody to watch Cache' so we can go out tonight?" My girl Brenda is going to meet us at the club." "Alright, I'm gone drop Cache' off by my mom on the way out."

Dionne put on her black Versace jumpsuit and her gold boots and then she made up her face. She got Cache' ready and dropped her off by her grandmother. Dionne and Ashley pull up in front the club and jumps out of Dionne's Cadillac truck. "What's up Brenda?" Ashley asks. "What you think is up booty nose. I'm waiting on your slow ass." "Come on let's go in." "You looking some sexy in your jump suit Dionne," Brenda commented. "Thanks Brenda this was a last minute outfit." "It's rolling in here this a hot spot," says Ashley.

"Yeah it really is," responds Dionne. Ashley and Dionne walk to the bar to get a drink and Brenda goes to the restroom to freshen up. "Grey goose and cranberry." "The same for me," Ashley adds. When the bartender put the drink on the bar a nice dressed guy tells the bartender, "I got that." "Thank you," Dionne says looking up at the guy with a smile. "What's your name beautiful?" "Dionne and you are?" "Malcolm, I think you look real nice and I love your big brown eyes. You think we can exchange numbers and call each other sometimes?" "Sure."

Brenda walks up to the bar and notices Will. Will walks straight up to the bar with his boys. He pulls out a handful of hundred dollar bills giving the bartender their orders. "Look at this fake bitch," says Brenda. "Who Brenda," Ashley ask?" Damn Ashley why, you don't miss a beat." "You're speaking out loud so I wanted to know who you were talking about hoe." " What Will played you because he's good at playing girls." "Yeah, I guess he did play me if he fucked me and threw me money for breakfast. That bitch hasn't answered his phone since." Ashley laughs out loud. "He's coming this way, Brenda act like you don't see him." "That's hard to do when he's looking directly at me." Will walks up with all his boys walks by Brenda. "What's up ladies? Ya'll chilling?" "We are," everyone responds. "Well, well, well," Will says looking over at Brenda. "I don't know what the hell you're looking at me for." "So we meet again, with your sexy ass." "What's good," Will ask? "Me not fucking with you how about that?" Brenda yells trying to talk over the music. All Will's boys look at him and bust out laughing. "What's up with the attitude Brenda," Will ask. "No attitude just mood swings." "What you doing after the club baby?" Will asks looking very interested. "Nothing" Brenda then smiles. "Maybe we can hook up after." "Alright Will I'll holler at you." I'll be waiting on your call. I'll see you later then." Brenda walks over to meet Dionne and Ashley by the DJ booth. "Are you having fun?" Brenda asks. "Yeah it's straight," Dionne replies. "Did you like the guy you met at the bar?" Brenda asks. "I did he was nice." Dionne goes on the dance floor with her drink in her hand and toots her booty in the air shaking her ass. "You know she's good for that." "Yeah she needed this," replies Ashley." With Ron gone she needs to come out and enjoy herself." "You right Brenda." Donald walks up watching Dionne dance. "Shake Dionne shake, I'm watching that ass," screams Donald. "Donald go sit your tired ass down somewhere," Ashley shouts. "I didn't know Dionne had it in her she's cutting up." "Whatever Donald," Dionne sighs.

Donald is Wills brother; he has money but not as much as his brother. Will is more out spoken; Donald is calm, cool and collective. He has another side if you cross him the wrong way. It is now two thirty and the club is ending. Everybody is walking out going to their cars and Brenda's phone rings. Brenda answers, "It's Brenda who's on my other line?" "This is Will who else you expecting to call your phone this time of morning?" "Nobody Will. What's up with you?" "You know I want to see you so don't get in the car with Dionne. I'm gone spend the bend and you jump in the car with me." "Alright Will hurry up." "I'll be there in a second be patient." Brenda hangs up the phone. Dionne and Ashley stares at Brenda. "Well, Ash how you like that? That hoe Brenda going do something nasty with that mouth tonight." "Shame on you," Ashley laughs. "What ya'll laughing at?" Brenda asks?" "I guess the joke is on you." "Ya'll damn right, I'm gone give big Will some so mind ya'll business. Brenda walks off to get in the car with Will. He was rolling in his candy apple red BMW Coupe. Brenda glances back at Ashley and Dionne saying, "Call ya'll tomorrow girlies."

CHAPTER VI

Dionne gets home and gets a phone call from Ron. "Press zero if you want to accept the call," the operator says on the other line. "What's up Dionne, what ya'll doing?" "Nothing Ron, we just walking inside." "Where ya'll coming from?" "Out and I'm getting ready for bed so I can get up in the morning." "I see you acting bad while I'm in here." "How I'm acting bad I've been faithful to you handling all you business paying for all your phone calls coming to see you and taking care of our daughter on my own by myself so why is it a problem when I go out once every blue moon Ron?" "Whatever Dionne, I don't understand why you have to go out if you not looking for nobody but fuck I'm just calling to let you know I'll be home soon." "Why you just now telling me?" I wasn't going to tell you at all. I wanted to come home and bust your ass." "Bust me doing what?" "I heard a lot of shit about you since I've been in here but it's cool." "Ron that's sad. You believe whatever bitches tell you. It's probably the same bitches you still fucking with telling you shit." "Yeah ok Dionne my phone is about to hang up I'll talk to you tomorrow and tell my baby Cache' I love her." "Whatever bye," Dionne hung up the phone and starred at the wall and thought about everything she did for Ron and he just acted unappreciative. Tears dropped from her eyes. All I did for him and I'm just finding out he's coming home. Dionne grabbed Cache' and laid down and telling her how much she meant to her. As Dionne dosed off, her phone rings. It's the guy she met at the club, Malcolm. "She was so tired she didn't answer. She decided that she would wait to talk to him tomorrow.

"Come on Brenda, do that for me. Come on make me feel good," says Will. Brenda strutted her way to the bed by Will. "Brenda that feels so good but don't go so hard your hurting it." Your mouth feels so warm," Will moan while pushing Brenda's head up and down. "Will, why you keep pushing my head like that?" "Brenda just do it, stop asking all them question, you fucking up the mood." "Who the hell you think you talking to?" "Bay come on." Brenda...turn over let me hit you from the back." Brenda turns over positioning her ass in the air and Will sticks himself in Brenda. "Yeah Will push harder and slap my ass." "That's right "B" back it up on that dick." "Brenda its coming!" "Yeah Will I'm coming too and it feel so uhhh!" Brenda collapsed on Will and fell asleep.

Chapter VII

Lily's phone rings. Lily jumps out the tub. She wraps the towel around her thinking why does my phone have to ring while I'm in the tub? Water was dripping all over the floor. "Hello." "Hey Lily what's up, what you doing?" "Nothing much getting out the tub." "Sasha and I are going to the Spa and we wanted to know if you wanted to come?" "Sure, I need a man to rub me down anyway. We haven't been with Sasha in a minute since she got married to that football player. They separated now though huh?" "Yeah, that's why she has time for us." "Right, so we have a chance to do some catching up. We're going to meet at Misty's Spa." "Ok Dee see you then."

William Sams wakes up to sunlight. "What time is it?" "Its ten thirty. Will what's wrong with you?" Brenda asked. "Nothing, but I do know I have to get the hell out of here. I have things to do." "Will it's always you have something to do. No breakfast no nothing you just get up and go." "Let's get something straight Brenda, you not my ole lady, you know what time of day it is when you come to the room with me. I'm tired of you questioning me about what I do. I'm not entitled to have breakfast with you so stop clouding me." "Oh, no the fuck you didn't." "Yes the fuck I did and here is some money for breakfast again." Will threw the money on the bed. "William how you could do this to me after you ask me to come here." "You right Brenda; I asked you I didn't beg you. You had a choice, you chose to come." "You so damn low down." "Well damn Brenda the world is not in your favor. That's the reason why I don't have an ole' lady because of bitches like you. I don't want to be questioned about nothing." Brenda was felt so low; all she could do was hold her head down. "Alright Will just go head, I'll catch a cab home." "Well, hit me up when you make it home." "Yeah right Will that's a complete joke." "Whatever Brenda, I'm out." *Man how much does a woman have to go through to realize when enough is enough.*

"Cache', Cache', get up honey we have to get dressed," Dionne screams while walking through the hall of their house. "Mom where do we have to go, I'm so tired." "I hear that your daddy is coming home today so I want to make sure us ladies are nice and pretty; while he's trying to sneak out on us." "Yea daddy's coming home, I'm so happy mom." "I know you are Cache', so lets start getting dress." "Ok mom but can I ask you something?" "Sure baby, you can ask me something." "Is daddy going to leave us again?" "You know honey, I hope he doesn't; we have to pray that daddy makes better decisions." "Sure mommy."

CHAPTER VIII

It's seven o'clock Tuesday morning. One by one ex-prisoners exit the gates. Ronald Darrell Brown walks out the gates of prison a freeman after four years. As the gates open Dionne and Cache' get out the car. When Cache' saw Ronald she ran up to him. "Daddy, daddy, hi daddy, I missed you so much." Dionne stands there with a smile on her face. "I missed ya'll too." "Ron, why did you try to keep this a secret from me?" "Keep what a secret?" "You coming home what's the point in you not telling me, you knew I would find out." "Well Dionne you know now so get over it. Come so I can go make some visits. Then we can go home and get our groove on."

Ashley calls Lily to update her about Ron's homecoming. "Hey Lily, what's up?" "Girl lying back on the couch watching television." "Pookie, I was calling to let you know that Mr. Ron came home today." "Really, Dionne didn't mention it to me." "Well from my understanding he didn't tell Dionne because he wanted to surprise her but you know somebody spilled the beans and told her anyway." "What did she say about that?" "She was very upset eventually she'll get over it." "That dude down bad for that." "Damn that craziness what Brenda tired ass been doing?" "That disturbed lil' hoe keep playing with Will's low down ass. Brenda acting like she then lost her mind behind his dog ass. You know his so call girlfriend busted them in Will's house." "Girl that's a shame what happened?" "They passed words bout to fight." He's not worth it men are going to what they want regardless. One woman is never enough for them. The sooner we realize that the better we would be." "That's the truth Lily. I'll call you later we need to get our crazy asses off this phone and do something with ourselves." "Got you Ash bye."

Ron and Dionne walk in the house after a day of visiting. Ron went to lay Cache' down in her bed and went back in the room with Dionne. Dionne comes out the shower with her robe on. She unties the robe as she blocks the T.V. standing directly in front of Ron with no clothes on. "You missed me baby?" "You know I did." "It was a long time me here all alone without you." Thoughts of her unfaithfulness ran through Dionne's head. "A long time missing Ron was true; being all alone was the lie." Ron started caressing Dionne's body up and down kissing her all over from her stomach to the mid part of her thigh. Ron's kisses aroused them both. "Are you liking the feeling?" Ron asks Dionne looking directly in her eyes. "Enjoying it," Dionne moaned. Ron sucked, kissed and licked so good on Dionne's pussy until she busted right in his mouth. Ron inserted himself in Dionne looking into her eyes and whispering in her ear, "It's been a long time Dee since I had this and it's even better than before." They sex all kinds of positions; positions Dionne never had knowledge of. She thought to herself this is the best sex ever. The sex ended doggie style with Ron cumin all over her butt. When they were finished, they were so overwhelmed from the intense love making they fell asleep naked holding each other tight.

CHAPTER IX

Will sent invitations to everybody he invited to his big birthday bash.

YOUR ARE CORDIALLY INVITED
TO ATTEND THE BIGGEST
BIRTHDAY BASH EVER.
GIVEN BY: WILLIAM SAMS
WHERE: 308 CADDY DR.
WHEN: SATURDAY
AFTER THIS FRIDAY
TIME: 10 PM TIL' YOU FALL.

"Hey Ashley," Brenda says when she walks in the nail shop. "What's up?" "Where you coming from?" "Oh a little bit of everywhere, I had to make a couple of runs this morning." "Real busy on a Saturday morning huh," Ashley asks? "Yes, I woke up to a delivery from a special man." "Oh really," Ashley laughs. "Yes, really." Ashley you didn't get a visit?" "A visit for what and from whom." "The special man that Will is sending around." "Brenda you to funny." "My bay bay is having a big birthday bash and he has this guy personally dropping off invitations to everybody that's on his guest list." "Are you serious? He's doing it like that?" "Yes, he is Ash and I wonder since you didn't get yours yet was I the first on his list. "Probably," Ashley replies. Why don't you call and ask him if you were." "Who you talk bout your boyfriends having he birthday party" the Chinese lady asks Brenda while she's polishing her nails. "Yes our boyfriends," Brenda answers. "Nosy ass," Brenda whispers to Ashley. "Her ass is nosy. Wont you go head and call Will." "Alright bitch I'll call and ask."

"Yeah who's this?" "Damn you forgot my number already." Brenda says in a pissed off tone. "It's you, is there something I can help you with?" "That's how the hell you talk to me when I call you?" "Fuck Brenda, you sure know how to blow a good high. What do you need I'm in the middle of something?" "What are you doing like that?" "First off Brenda, we already went through this you not my ole' lady, so I really don't owe you no explanation. I know you didn't call for all this. So what's the real reason you called?" "Why you talking to me like this Will?" "When we together it's something different." "Your pussy so good Brenda, I can't resist it when I'm with you." "So that's what it's about, my pussy?" Will laughs, "Nah baby." "I was calling to tell you I received my invitation to your big birthday bash and I just wanted to know was I first on your guest list." "Now come on Brenda, you already know you didn't even have to call me and ask that crazy question." "I just wanted to know Will because Ashley says she didn't get hers yet so I was curious to know." "Well bay, tell Ashley she should be getting hers shortly but my good stuff had to get hers first." "I'll let her know." "Don't be calling me like that tripping for nothing. That's business on the other line, I'll talk to you later." "Alright baby, bye." Brenda hangs up the phone. "Girl that boy is a mess." "He really is" Ashley responds. "Who you boyfriend?" The Chinese lady asks again. "Yeah my boyfriend" Brenda smirks as she and Ashley walk out the nail shop. "Damn the Chinese lady all up in our business. I wanted to tell her no he you man." "Girl you are so silly," Ashley says laughing.

"Ron home huh," Ashley ask Brenda? "Yes I hear he's home but I haven't heard anything about him and Dionne thus far." "Well Ashley, I'll talk to you later since I have to go to the mall and find something sexy to wear to my baby birthday bash." "I feel you miss Will, I'll talk to you when I get off tonight.

CHAPTER X

Dionne wakes up Cache'. "Get up Cache', it's time to start getting ready for school." Still laying in her princess bed Cache' responds, "Uh, mom, do I have to go to school today?" "Yes Princess, you have to get up so daddy can bring you to school." "Hurry up and brush your teeth and wash your face darling, so you can come get dress." "Ok, mom." "Ron get up," Dionne calls out. "Yeah alright Dionne." "Good morning daddy. Mommy I'm done I'm ready to get dress." "Good morning my baby daddy's happy to see you." "Same here daddy." "Girl you know you something else." Dionne smiles at Cache'. "Boy get up so ya'll can go." "I'm about to stop damn rushing me." "What?" Dionne yells. "You heard me," Ron says as he stumps off. This bastard is tripping Dionne thought to herself. "Bye mommy" Cache' says. "Bye momma baby. I'll see you after school. Love you." "Love you to mom." "Ron make sure you don't leave until she gets in the building." "Yes ma'am."

Ron drops Cache' off at school and gets a phone call. "Hello." "What's up baby where you at?" "Just dropping my daughter off at school." "Where she at?" "She's at home." "So that means your passing over here." "Yeah give me about thirty minutes; I have to make a stop." "Just call me when you on your way." "Fo Sho."

Lily is banging so hard on Sasha's door. "Who is it knocking on my door like your crazy?" "Open the damn door it's freezing out here." Sasha opens the door. "I should've left you out there to freeze the way you're banging on my door." "Don't play with me trick." Lily walks in Sasha's house and goes straight in the kitchen. "I'll be back down Lily." "What you have a dick up there?" "Yes, I do and don't disturb us." "Well shit I'll

35

come back; you don't have any here for me?" "Girl I'm just playing I wish." "Sasha don't play games like that hot ass." "I am hot but I can use a dildo to get my satisfaction," Sasha says. "Ha, ha you are stupid girl." "I'm going run upstairs and brush my teeth. You can go in the kitchen and make yourself useful and fix us breakfast." "Are you kidding bitch, no problem." Sasha phone rings and Lily answers the phone. "Who's this?" "Hi can I speak with Sasha." "Who's calling?" "Jeffery, who am I speaking with?" "This is the one and only Lily." "Lily, how are you?" "I'm fine Jeffery and you?" "I'm good thanks for asking is Sasha available?" "No I'm sorry Lily says, but she's taking a shower I can have her call you or you can call her back in fifteen minutes." "Will do, thanks Lily." "No problem." "Who was that on the phone Lily?" Sasha asks walking down the steps. "That was someone by the name of Jeffery." "Jeffery my baby; why didn't you call me to the phone?" "I thought you were in the shower." "No bitch, you know I told you I was going to brush my teeth that don't sound close to going take a shower." "Alright Sasha I got confused. He's calling you back in fifteen minutes calm down." "Anyway what are we having for breakfast?" "I got eggs and bacon frying, biscuits in the oven with our juice on counter." "Good Lily by the way have you spoken to Dionne today?" "No but I heard through the grape vine that Ron was messing with his baby momma and some other stink bitch." "Girl really and that nigga haven't been home two months and he's starting his shit pass me the grape jelly." "Believe me Sasha, Dionne will find out." "I know that's the truth." While Lily and Sasha is at the table eating breakfast Sasha door bell rings.

Now who could this be uninvited? "Who is it? With your uninvited self?" "This is the special delivery man I have a drop off." What could he possibly be dropping off that's so important that it had to be special delivered?" Sasha said hitting Lily on the arm. "I don't damn know but if you open the door we can find out." Lily pulls the door open wide with her hands on her hip shaking her leg. "I have something for Sasha" the delivery man says." "That would be her Lily says pointing in Sasha direction." "Good can you just sign here stating that you received this?" "Sure special delivery man. Right here?" "Yes, ma'am." "Thanks Ms. Sasha." "You're welcome." Sasha closes the door opening the envelope. "What is it?" Lily screams. It reads you are invited to the Biggest Birthday Bash Given by William "Will" Sams. "What Sasha, Will is given a birthday bash?" "Yes he is Lily." "What are we going to wear to this party?" "Don't know yet." You best believe it'll be nice and sexy." "Word Sasha." Lily yells slapping Sasha hand.

CHAPTER XI

Dionne and Ashley meets up at Misty's Spa so they can go shopping for an outfit for Will's birthday bash. Dionne pulls up in her new pearl white Range Rover blowing her horn. "Ash you can ride with me and leave your car parked here." "Good, cause I really didn't feel like driving anyway." Ashley hops in the truck with Dionne. "Dionne this truck is hot when you got this?" "Yesterday on the expense of Ron." "That's what I'm talking bout, where is your beautiful daughter?" "She's by my momma, they going to the zoo today." "How's Ron?" "He's good; he's out at the mall looking for something to wear to the party." "You have something in mind you want to wear?" "Not really," Dionne replies." "But whatever I wear, I'ma make sure Ron will want to come home and get right in me," Ashley laughs. "Why all my friends have to be so out spoken?" "I don't know you know what they say "Birds of a feather flock together!" They both laugh and Dionne turns up the music.

"What up Mr. Ronald?" Will say as he walks up to Ron dapping him off. "Not a damn thing." "Are you coming to the party?" "Yeah, you know I'll be there." "Good, good. What's' been up with you since you been home, it's been a minute huh?" "Yep, I've just been chilling laying low." "The family, Cache', Dionne, how are they?" "They're good." "Ron I heard you been hollin' at your girl Shannon and you back playing with Nicollet." "Yeah man I pass through sometimes to give them a sample." "They both gone be at the party so keep it cool." "I got you. I'll catch up with you later Will I need to go finish looking for an outfit for your big party." "That's what's up peace."

"Hey Lily this Dionne; what time you think you'll be ready for me to pick you up because I invited my new friend to come with us if you didn't mind." "No I don't mind but what new friend?" "Kimora, the lady I told you I met at Starbuck's the other day. It was just something about her. It was like a vibe I got from her. Her spirit instantly connected us. You know Lily people have spirits that can jump on you some can be good and some can be bad and I felt a good spirit from her." "Really Dionne." "Yes ma'am, you'll meet her soon." "Well Lily so much for that I'll be there around nine." "Alright." "Make sure you're cute Lily." "You already know how I roll cute and sexy is the only two things that describes me." "I know miss stuck on yourself," Dionne says as she hangs up the phone. Ron busts through the door with lots of bags in his hand. He drops them everywhere making all kind of noise. "Ronald what's wrong with you?" "What you mean what's wrong with me?" "What's wrong with you and your little attitude slamming bags everywhere?" "I don't have an attitude and where you think your going?" "The same place you're going to Will's birthday bash." "What you going for Dionne?" "What kind of damn question is that? The same reason your going." "Dionne you don't need to go." "Oh yeah, well I'm going and that's a done deal." "What?" "You need to stay your ass home." "Alright Ronald whatever."

"Sasha girl how does this look?" "It's nice, but you look like you went found the shortest shorts there was." "I did honey, this is the party for whom? William my man Sams." "Your man Brenda be for real how many women you think he has?" "One as far as I'm concerned, me." "If you say so." "I'm saying because I know so." Sasha laughs, "Alright Mrs. Sams." "That's right now let's go we have people to meet and greet." Kahlil pulls up by Ron blowing his horn non-stop. Ron in the bathroom mirror doing his final touches. "Who is blowing the horn like they crazy?" Dionne says with anger in her voice. "That's my ride; I'm on my way out." "You're getting all clean and fresh and think I'm staying home? I don't even think so." "We'll see Dionne, don't play with me." "I'm out," Ron sighs. Dionne says under her breath bye he's out huh. I'm going to show him who's staying home. I don't know who he thinks he is." Dionne jumps in the shower to get ready for the party.

Will is running around the house making sure everything is in place before his guest start arriving. Will yells down the hall to Donald to see what time security will get to the house. "I just hung up with them Will, they're checking in at the gates." "Great, Donald is the caterers in there places and the bartenders on point?" "Everyone's in place," Donald confirms. "Fantastic, are the buses in place to pick up the guest? I swear I don't want all those damn cars parked on my property." "I got you now go sit you're nervous ass down." "I'm about to go get cleaned up, take care the rest Donald my boy." "I told you I got you Will my boy."

CHAPTER XII

Dionne gets her Prada purse from out the top of her closet and put all her personal things in it. She slips her feet in her Prada boots to cover her jeans, and heads out to her car. Dionne dials Kimora's number, "Hey Kimora this Dionne." "Hi Dionne, what's going on?" "I'm leaving out my garage and I'm on my way. I should be by you, let's say in about twenty minutes. I'll pick you up first and then we can go get Lily." "I'll be ready by time you get here." Dionne turned her radio up listening to I can't stand the rain by Seal. I would love to know what Ron's trip was about today Dionne thought as she drives off.

Brenda and Sasha pulls up to a unique place that looks like a theater where all kinds of cars were pulling up parking and buses were picking people up. "Brenda, Brenda, there is definatley a lot of people up in here." Yes, Brenda agrees nodding her head. "Your man is doing it big!" "He is right Sasha?" "He sure needs to be giving me some of that big money," Brenda said with excitement. "You sure need to be asking for it," Sasha says grinning as they get on the bus. "These men sure smell good making my pussy cut up," says Sasha sniffing the aroma. "Control yourself Sasha." "Yeah if you say so."

Lamar hollers upstairs to Will, "William Sams are you ready? Your guests are starting to arrive." "Almost ready just let the butlers greet them and bring them to their area. When I'm about to come down I'll text you and let you know so the D.J. can make the announcement." "I'm going to do just that Will." Lamar walks by the D.J. and informs him about Will's announcement when most of his guest start to arrive. "The pleasure is mine," D.J. Rob confirms.

When the bus with Brenda and Sasha pulled up their eyes got big. "This is beautiful," Sasha says to Brenda. The pine tress in front of Will's house was gorgeous Sasha thought to herself. As they walked up to Will's house there was a waterfall with colorful rocks and two huge iron gates that opened on both sides. The guest were greeted in front the gates. The butlers were dressed in black suits with rust shirts shaking the guest hands and showing them what directions to go in. People were showing up at the same time walking from different angles. "Brenda this is set up so pretty, I must say he did his thing." "Girl Sasha it is and Will has all kinds of cars a Benz Coupe, Land Rover and a Bentley parked in front his gigantic house. "That's nice when you have it like that. Shit, I know that's too much for my pockets." "It is I must agree Sasha."

As you entered the house there were more greeters that greeted you with a glass of Chrystal. Brenda and Sasha grab a glass of champagne sipping it. "This champagne is mighty rich Brenda." "Do you know where you at?" a man whispered to Sasha as he over heard Sasha comment about the champagne. "At William Sam's party right? As if Sasha forgotten. "Top of the class everything that's all he knows." "Is that right sir? I' am kind of confused of where I'm at but sir I appreciate you reminding me," Sasha says laughing as her and Brenda walks off from the guy. As you walk further back there's sticks everywhere burning fire, party lights flashing. A jazz band playing in the middle part of the yard. The DJ is set up in the last part of the yard. Brenda and Sasha spots Dionne and Lily coming through the door. "Here comes your friends and they look like they have somebody new with them." Brenda whispers to Sasha. "Hi ladies," Lily says to Sasha and Brenda with a smile. "Hello women," Sasha and Brenda reply. "Kimora this is Brenda and Sasha and ya'll this is Kimora." "Nice to meet ya'll." Kimora says with a hand shake. "Everything is so nice," Kimora shouts trying to talk over the music. "Let's go walk to the yard to see who else may be here," Dionne signals to the ladies. Lamar, Ron, Donald and their friends all are standing around the pool talking. "Man, look at all these fine ass women in here" Donald says happy hugging Lamar around the shoulders. "Yes, they do man and look there go two of your women Ronald, Shannon and Nicollet." "Yeah, I see them Lamar." "Where is Dionne your main woman?" "I told her to stay her ass at home." "Why is that?" Lamar questioned. "She doesn't need to be here." "Oh yeah, because you knew your other women were going to be here." "Is yours here Lamar," Ron asked agitated? "Say bra' we're going to leave that alone." "Yeah let's leave that alone."

Nicollet walks up to the group of guys. "Hey Ronald, what's up with you?" "Nothing Nicollet where's my son?" "He's by my brother. You could have called him today." "I was doing a lot of running today." "Yeah, I know you always have an excuse." "Nicollet don't start your shit. Go head with that." While Ronald and Nicollet were passing words Dionne and her girls walk in the second yard area. Ron eyes got real big. "I'll talk to you later because I don't have the patience for her to come over here playing with me." "You know Nicollet I think that's a good idea, Donald says. "What the fuck is she doing here?" "You not talking about Dionne huh," Donald says as he sipped his drink. Here come your girl let me move from over here before she comes punch the piss out you." "Real funny Donald or you got jokes?" Ron says, pissed off at Donald comment. "I run this shit not Dionne." "I heard that" Lamar laughs.

May I have everybody attention the D.J. yells in the mic. The moment we've been waiting for the birthday boy is on his way out. Introducing the one and only Mr. William Dejaun Sams a Native American still looking good at twenty eight and enjoy life to the fullest can come on out. Will steps out dressed all hot with his jewelry on. It was sparkling like crazy. The DJ played the "President is black" by Young Jeezy and William came out smiling from ear to ear. Brenda notice while everybody was screaming, whistling and clapping some woman steps up by the stage with a lil short Paris Hilton type dress smiling and shaking her head at Will clapping in slow motion. "Who's that bitch?" Brenda thought to herself. What I guess he's fucking her too. "Brenda, you ok?" Sasha asks as she notices Brenda with a vicious look on her face. "No I'm not, do you see that whore standing by the stage watching Will like she can't wait for the party to be over with so she can get something started." Far as I'm concerned nobody will be fucking him tonight but me." I guess "B" you're sure about that?" "Yes, I'm damn sure about that Sasha." "Okay, honey don't get hostile keep your cool." "I am cool."

"I hope ya'll are enjoying yourselves and please at the end of the party don't forget to pick up your gift bags." William says before he walks off the stage. Brenda hurries up and walks up to Will before the other lady gets to him. "Hey Will." "Hey Brenda what's up?" "Nothing much." "You look nice William." "You do to Brenda; thank you for coming out to my party?" "No problem Will." "What are you planning on doing after your party?" "I don't really know what you're trying to give me some?" "You know it, I really miss it." "I'll let you know what's up." As Brenda and Will were ending their conversation the girl that Brenda notice by the stage walked up. "Hi Will baby the lady says wrapping her arms around Will's neck." "Hi Akira what's good with you?" "You baby you." Will grins, "Let's step over here Akira. Brenda I'm gone to holler at you before the party ends." "Yeah whatever Will," Brenda says fired up. "I can't believe that bitch!" "Fuck him."

"Dionne you still came to the party after I ask you not to come." "Well if you would have stayed home Ron then I would have joined you." "You can't do what I do Dionne." "That's one of your rules Ron?" Dionne asks turning towards the pool guests were jumping in. "Now I see your damn baby momma is here that's why you didn't want me to come." Nicollet looked over her shoulder when she passed Ron and Dionne and over heard Dionne speaking out loud. "I knew she was going to be here that's why I came." "Now you watch my ass go side to side while your looking at that trash out the corner of your eyes." Dionne twists off in her fitted True Religion jeans. "Who is that sexy fine ass man right there?" Lily asks pointing towards Lamar. "Girl that's Lamar big fine ass," Ashley responds. "Yeah, I want to meet him." "You do Lily?" "Yes." "I'll introduce ya'll later." "Alright honey I'm going to hold you to that." "You got it."

The party is almost over and the DJ is making his final announcements. "Last round for drinks at the bar. Hennessy shots at the bar are going fast." The guest just went swarming to all three bars. "Is that you Mr. Sexy big abs Lamar?" "That would be me Ashley, how are you?" "I'm good my friend Lily wants to say hi." "One shot of Patron," Lamar ordered. "What's good with you Ms. Lily?" "Nothing much?" "Are you enjoying the party?" "I am do you have a girlfriend Lamar?" "No I don't and you?" "No sir, single as single can be." "Let's exchange numbers and we can get to know each other." "Lily, holler at me." "You got that." "See Lily that was easy right?" "It was Ashley," Lily says with a smile. "Come on girl lets go catch up with the rest of the girls since the party is almost over."

"Where the hell ya'll been?" Sasha says slurring. "In the back," Kimora replies, looking confused. "Are you ok Sasha?" Lily asks sarcastically. "Yeah I'm straight." "You look like you drunk a little too much." "Uh huh, ya'll need to worry about them dog ass fools you and Dionne have." Dionne minding her own business turns around. "What the fuck are you talking about bitch?" "Yeah some of them hoes face you smile in knows that Ron is fucking back with Nicollet and messing with that stink bitch Shannon." "What are you talking about?" "Why don't you ask that whore Brenda." "Damn you Sasha with your immature ass. I know you have issues so I'm going to go there with you." "What's wrong Brenda did Will push you to the side to play with Barbie?" "You know what Sasha I'm gone excuse you tonight because

I know you been drinking but other than that I would kick your ass." "Yeah right Brenda, remember when you're drunk you speak a sober mind. Well personally I will be finding this shit out," Dionne says angrily.

The DJ started playing second line music with fireworks going off in the air. A sign flying in the sky over us saying, *THANKS FOR COMING OUT.* The DJ then announced, "Don't forget to pick up your goodie bags on your way out I hear there's a lot of great things in there."

CHAPTER XIII

William Sams was standing at the gate as his guest were leaving along with Donald and Lamar giving out the bags and also telling everyone thanks for coming. As Brenda was leaving she walks to the gate where Will was standing. "Nice party Will." "Thanks again Brenda glad you enjoyed it." "So are we going to hook up tonight?" "I'm going to call you Brenda and let you know." "Now you're going to call me any other time you can give me an answer with no hesitation." "Your right but tonight I'm going to call you, you heard me?" Will sees Akira walking up and starts brushing Brenda off. Brenda looks back wondering why Will went into a zone. "Is this another one you fucking Mr.Sams?" "Fucking?" Who else other than her I'm fucking Brenda?" "What is going on?" Akira asks pissed off as she notices Will and Brenda passing words. "You stay the fuck out of this, I'm talking to him." Sasha and Lily are grabbing Brenda telling here to come on don't worry about it. "No fuck that who is she Will?" "That's my fucking ole' lady." "Your ole' lady where is your ole lady when you're renting rooms for us so we can have our fuck time." "Will what the hell is this hoe talking about?" "Your man a hoe bitch." "I don't damn know what she's talking about but she better get somewhere." Donald, Lamar and Ron looking in amused. "No I'm not going anywhere until you apologize to me." "Apologize, bitch please. You can step right off my property. Security help her possessive ass to the bus." "You better remember this," Brenda says screaming with hurt and embarrassment. "Goodnight and Will walked off to his house. Akira ran off behind Will to get more information on the situation. "Will what was that all about?" "Look Akira, I don't want to here that shit in m ear." "What? This lady just disrespected me and this is all you can say to me?" "If you keep asking me stupid ass questions I'm going to say nothing to you." "Bastard who do you think you are?" Mr. William "Will" Sams. "Do you fuck with that bitch?" "Do you fuck with me?" "I'm not joking Will." "I'm not either leave me alone about that I'm going take a shower meet me in the room." Akira just set on the big puff leather sofa thinking to herself, this kind of shit right will make a woman cheat on their mate.

CHAPTER XIV

Dionne made it home before Ron. She got into her see through lingerie and sprayed on her Vanilla Noir. "Can't wait for him to get home so we can make love." It feels so good to finally lie in my big comfortable bed. Ron walks in the house about thirty minutes after Dionne. "You're already ready for me?" "Yes I am." "Why did you come to the party after I told you not to come?" "Are you serious Ron?" "Yes I am you need to do as I ask or else it will turn out bad." "What is that suppose to mean Ron?" "Don't worry about that Dionne, now come give me some head." Dionne slowly moved from the top of the bed putting on Brandy song 'Human' and then she met Ron at the end of the bed and grabbed his dick rubbing it up and down and she started licking the top of his head and stroking his balls. She put his dick in her mouth, and went to sucking it. Ron moans, "uh yeah baby watch your teeth, use your lips." Ron started pushing Dionne head up and down. Dionne asks Ron "like this baby?" Just like that bay, Ron answers." Ron turned Dionne over and wiggles his tongue on her pearl tongue. Dionne pussy was soak and wet and Ron sucked all of her wetness. He then inserted himself in her moaning loud, "This is the best pussy I've ever had you are so warm inside." "I love this pussy" Ron was yelling as he was pounding Dionne. Ron begins to go harder and harder and deeper and deeper. Dionne clinched Ron back, leaving scratches all over it. "I'm about to catch an orgasm," Dionne yells. Ron whispers in Dionne's ear, "I'm about to nut too." As they both came to their peak they held each other tight until they both climaxed. "Dee that shit was so good." "You too!" Dionne kisses Ron on the lips and tells him,

"If you fuck over me you would really hurt me!" "I won't hurt you", Ron responds. I'm curious of who Shannon is and hears that your playing with Nicolette. Dionne whispered as she turned over to go to sleep. Ron starred up at the ceiling stunned, "Where did she get that information from?"

Lily calls Lamar the next evening after she met him at the party. "Hey Lamar it's me Lily from the party." "Yeah I remember you; I remember you from the party." "What are you getting into today?" "Nothing much Lily, how about we go get a drink at Cannon's house?" "That's cool I'll see you there about sixish." "Yes, good timing Lamar I'll see you then." "Make sure your looking sexy for me." "Anything for your fine ass." Lamar started blushing.

"Sasha that bitch Will is a low down nigga," Brenda says in disappointment. "Well Brenda where you fucked up at is involving your feelings in your massacred," Sasha says. "Like that never happened to you before Sasha." "I never said it didn't but I did learn from my mistakes. As a friend that's why I'm trying to help you with involving your feelings with a man that you know have a family already and have a lot of female friends." "It wasn't something I was able to control it just happened and he lied and told me he didn't have a woman." " You know we all lie when we really want to try somebody I don't care if your man or woman but Brenda if you just go in like a man that don't care just coming in to fuck no strings attached then you'll be alright but if you go in with your heart that's when it becomes a problem for that person who feelings is deeper. You will get hurt in the long run." "Your right Sasha, so what do you do if you're already there?" "What you mean there?" Sasha asked. "When your heart is involved." "When you know it's not right you let it go and take it to God in prayer. Ask him to take the burden off you." "Thanks for your advice Sasha, I really appreciate it." "Your welcome, anytime sweetie" replies Sasha. "Goodnight, Sasha long night I'm bout to get some rest," says Brenda.

Lamar and Lily meet up at the Cannon's house to have a drink. Lamar is at the table waiting for Lily. Lily walks in ten minutes later with a pair of tights on to show her shape, and a shirt hanging off one shoulder that went right past her butt and some BCBG heels. "Mmm you look mighty nice Lily and you smell some good with your fine ass," Lamar comments. "Thanks Lamar, Lily says with a smile. "You're looking mighty fine too with your tight Ed Harley shirt on, showing all your abs." "I wore this just for you," Lamar says. "Yeah I know you so sweet." "You must work out a lot huh Lamar?" "I do once I get off from work." "Where do you work?" "I travel to different cities driving trucks." "That's good," Lily says. "What about you?" What you do?" "I work at a reporting company. I do interviews and a couple of other things." "I got you; you talk to the famous that's good." Something like that anyway you have any kids Lamar?" "I have one four year old son, what about you?" "None at the moment but I treat my two friends kids like their mine." "Dinner was delicious; do you want to come to my place?" Lily asks. "Sure if you want me to." "I would love for you to come over." "I'll follow you then." Lamar gets in his silver Benz E350. "This is nice honey really nice." "Thanks, Lily now go get in your car.

Dionne gets home and lays Cache' in her bed. Dionne went into a transition. It is one in the morning. I wonder where Ron at. Dionne lay in her bed shaking her leg wondering where Ron could be. The thought came across her mind could he be either by Nicollet or Shannon. She could not get the thought out her mind. It is now five in the morning and Dionne hears keys rattling to enter the house. Ron walks in the home with not a worry on his mind. "Where the fuck have you been and why are you coming in my house at five in the morning?" "Stop fucking nagging me Dionne, Ron yells. "Excuse me? You're disrespecting my house and you have the nerve to tell me stop damn nagging you." Dionne screams. "Where have you been?" I ask. "Again, none of your fucking business." Dionne jumps out the bed with frustration from what Ron just said to her. She started pointing her finger in his face fussing. "I'm telling you Dionne get the fuck out my face." "You come in my house mid-morning and want to curse me out when I didn't do you nothing bitch." Before you knew it, Ron grabbed Dionne hair slammed her on the bed and started chocking and slapping her in the face. "Bitch, I asked you to leave me alone but you wouldn't listen." Dionne started screaming and crying. "You are wrong she shouted you came in here mid-morning acting like you're out working." "I was taking care of business." "Yeah right you're out there fucking with them hoes. One of them must have pissed you off and you want to take it out on me." "Shut up bitch you don't know what the fuck you talking about." "Stop it Ron you're hurting me." Cache' runs into the room and sees her daddy hitting her mom and Dionne yelling. "Stop

57

it daddy stop and get off momma," Cache' yells. Ron jumps off Dionne snatches Cache' and brings her back to her room. Dionne balls up on the bed crying so hard asking herself what I did to deserve this. When she got up to go to the bathroom, she noticed one side of her face swollen and puffy. "Oh my God how am I going to go around people looking like this?" Dionne just lay back down in her bed and cried harder.

CHAPTER XV

Lily and Lamar are drinking Raspberry Absolute getting twisted. Lamar took off his shirt flexing his abs for Lily. "Boy please stop doing that you have all my inside getting super wet." Lamar started smiling showing his pretty white teeth. "Hey, baby can you put on that new Jamie Fox so we can get more acquainted." "I love that idea Lamar anything for you." "Now Lamar are you sure you don't have a girlfriend or a wife? I don't have time for nobody to be calling my phone playing with me behind you." "What did I tell you Lily, I don't have one of those." "Alright then Lamar." "Now stop bringing that up and come give daddy a kiss." Lily walks over and sits on Lamar's lap. She puts her arms around his neck and stared into his eyes with passion. She leaned towards Lamar and started kissing his chest. Lamar grabbed Lily breast and put them in his mouth sucking them real good. "What kind of cologne you have on baby?" "It's called Bond #9." "What kind of spanish shit is that?" "Not spanish expensive baby girl." "Smells so good and boy your body is so fine I love your tattoos." "You do baby?" Lamar asks softly. "Yes baby, can you suck my titties some more that make me so hot." Lamar pushed Lily breast together messaging them and put them back in his mouth and started sucking them just as Lily asked. "Come get on top Lily." Lily positions herself and stretches her legs open and lands right on the tip of Lamar dick head. "Yeah bay go up and down on that dick and stand on your toes." Lily got on her toes and started going up and down and around to Lamar's satisfaction. Lily notices his toes curling. Uhh moans Lamar, "That's what I'm talking about. Turn over and bounce that ass for me so I can see how that dick look going in and out that pussy." "How does it feel?" Lily asks Lamar. "It feels too good," Lamar answers. "This is the best pussy I've ever had." Lamar picked Lily up and pressed her on the wall pushing inside her even harder. "Lamar it hurts slow down," Lily cries out. Ugh, moans Lamar as he came to his climax. Afterward they hugged each other and laughed. "Did you enjoy it?" Lily asked curiously. "I really did," Lamar answers while slowing down his breathing. Lamar lay on his back took his condom off and threw it in the toilet and flushed it.

Will and Donald took a ride to Florida for a two day vacation to visit some of their homies. "Will bra, what was up with your girl Brenda at the party she was tripping." "She was I put this good dick on her and now she don't know how to act." Will says as he and Donald start laughing. "That bitch got some good ass pussy I must admit." "Man your ass wild." "Just telling you the truth, I don't have to lie all the time." "What about Akira?" "What about her? She's going to accept whatever I give because she knows that nobody else gone take care of her like I do." "Yes indeed Will you're a pimp." "I get it from you it runs in our blood what can I say." "The party turned out real nice big brother." "It did I heard a lot of hating ass people was so concerned about what was in the gift bags. The Louis Vutton Key chains, Channel wallets, Marc Jacobs's cologne for the men and Dolce and Gabbana perfume for the women had their heads hurting. I leave them haters in the back seat while I push my ride." "That's what's up," Donald yelled. "I'm about to call Brenda," Will suggested. "Hello may I help you?" "What's up Brenda baby?" "Nothing." "Why are you being so sarcastic?" "Only with you," "Alright I'm sorry about the other night. You know you're my baby and that's my pussy." "I am Will?" "Fo Sho "B." When I get back in town I'm gone get at you." "What are you going out of town for Will to spend quality time with one of your women?" "Nah beautiful I have to take care of some business." "I'll be waiting Will for you to get back." "See Donald I got that shit on lock," Will says as he hangs up the phone. "I see big brother," Donald replies.

Dionne how are you doing? I haven't heard from you in a minute," Kimora asks sounding concerned. "I'm okay just been going through a lot." Deep inside Dionne knew she was hurting and she closed herself from the outside world. "A lot like what Dionne?" "Nothing serious but I'm getting better. I'll call you Kimora once I feel better ok." "Alright Dionne." Kimora hangs up the phone.

Ron stomps in the house screaming. Dionne got nervous shaking on the inside. "Where's my shit?" Ron yells while slamming the draws. "What shit?" Dionne asks furiously. "My shit," yells Ron. "I don't know what you're talking about. "What's wrong with you? "You're acting like your fucking somebody else because you have a whole new attitude." "So who you dealing with?" "I'm not dealing with no fucking body." "Why are you coming in here picking with me for nothing?" "Bitch shut the fuck up," Ron screams. "Fuck you Ron; I'm tired of this bullshit with you." Ron runs by Dionne and grabs her by her hair and drags her through the house hitting her. "What the fuck is wrong with you Ron? Do you get some type of enjoyment beating me? What did I do?" "Bitch you talk too much you just need to shut the fuck up." Cache runs in the room when she hears all the commotion and sees her daddy hitting her mom and screams, "Daddy stop you're scaring me." "You know what Dionne; I'm getting the fuck I'm leaving." "Why, so you can go be with your bitches?" Dionne says. "Yeah alright whatever you say." Cache is in her room with her head under her pillow scared to death. Ron packs his clothes and tries to leave; Dionne blocks the door grabbing Ron's things shouting, "You're not going anywhere. You promised me when you were in jail that you would never leave us and you need to keep your promise." Ron looked at Dionne crying in so much pain. He walked back in the room, and sat on the bed holding his head in his hands. Dionne went in the room with Cache holding her telling her everything is going to be alright and she kissed her on her forehead.

CHAPTER XVI

Lily and Lamar had gotten really comfortable with one another to the point they were spending all their time together. It's late in July and Lily and Ashley are going to an Aloha at the park giving by Donald. "Girl Lamar and I been kicking it hard. He's cool people I think I'm starting to fall for his fine ass." "He is fine. That he is!" Ashley responds. "I know girl I'm about to call him to see if he's coming to the aloha." "Hello," the lady on the other end says when she answers Lamar's phone. "Who is this?" "Who did you call for?" "I was calling for Lamar but I guess I got the wrong number," Lily says. No honey you dialed the right number this is Lamar's phone. He's at home resting from an all night flight; would you like to leave a message?" "Nah, who are you?" "I'm Tyra, Lamar's girlfriend." Lily damn near choked. "Girlfriend, Lamar never told me he had a girlfriend. He told me he was single." "Really, well we been together for over two years." "What, girl these dudes are so sad I've been dealing with him a few months now. "Where you been at? We fuck in the car, on the beach, at my house. As a matter of fact, I just slept by him two days ago and we fucked. Whenever we feel like fucking we fuck. He do me and I do him if you know what I mean I'm pregnant for him" Lily says looking at Ashley laughing under her breath. "Are you serious?" Tyra asks with disappoint in her voice?" "Yes I am so serious. The funny part about this is me not being told about a girlfriend." "Hilarious but I'll tell him his baby mother called." "You know Tyra, I really respect you because some of these hoes be trying to go off behind these no good ass men and be ready to fight the female instead of the person who's responsible for it all. We as women only go by what the man tells us. So my thing is why we should beef with each other it makes no sense." "Your right Lily, but if you still want to fuck with him that's on you because Lamar is going to continue to do what he wants to do anyway." "No chick I don't have time to deal with those types of situations." Lily hangs up her phone laughing with Ashley. "I guess he wont be attending the aloha. Tyra bout to go beat that ass especially when I said I'm pregnant lying my ass off." "That's what he get want to fucking cheat."

Lily parked her truck as they pulled up to the aloha. "Girl get out the car Lamar is not even a chapter anymore. This aloha going down." "Ah yeah" Lily throws her hands up singing, *What's your name girl, I'm so attracted to you.*" Lily started singing even louder that's what I'm talking about baby; they come a dime a second." Ashley started running through the sprinkling water.

Kimora bangs on Dionne's door and then continuously rings the doorbell. "Who's there?" Says Dionne through the speaker. "Me Kimora." "I'll be right down." Dionne opens the door with her pajamas on and her slippers. "Good evening Dionne." "Hi Kimora, what's going on?" "Nothing much are you going to the splash Dionne?" "I don't know Kimora, Ron already left to go." "Where's Cache'?" "By the babysitter Ron bought her over there this morning." "Well you need to go girl." "I've been feeling kind of sick weak, nausea, tired constantly, and always wanting to lay down." "Girl you might be pregnant again." "That's what I was thinking." "Take a pregnancy test." Kimora suggested. "I have one." "Take it then." Dionne went to the bathroom and peed in the cup and took the dropper and dripped the urine on the test. Dionne stood there nervously. The lines were turning pink slowly and finally the test read positive. Dionne put her head on the sink. "I am pregnant again for Ron." When Dionne walked out the bathroom Kimora jumped off the sofa. "So what is it friend?" "I'm pregnant, Kimora." "You are? So what are you going to do?" "I'm thinking about having an abortion." "Baby that's a no no if I have to help you with it I will. So get ready to have your baby that's going to have a long tooth when it's born coming out saying baby need a dentist." "You are stupid Kimora. I know, now lets go with your baby in the oven." Kimora says laughing.

Tyra pulls up to Lamar's house mad as hell. I would love to know what he has to say about this Lily person. Tyra slammed her door and marched up the steps. She put the keys in the door and turned the lock. Tyra put her purse and keys on the counter top and went straight to Lamar's room. When she opened the door Lamar was sound to sleep looking like a worry wasn't on his mind. Lamar, Lamar wake up," Tyra was saying pushing Lamar on his shoulder. "What the hell is wrong with you pushing me like your crazy." "Excuse me, what's wrong with me? What is wrong with you is the question? Who the heck is Lily?" Lamar jumped up with a confused look on his face. "Say again." "You heard me who the hell is Lily that called your phone saying she messes with you and she's pregnant with your child?" Where is my phone?" Lamar asks while moving his covers around. Tyra threw Lamar's phone to him. "Here's your damn phone." Lily told me that ya'll been kicking it for a minute. Is that true?" "No, that's true and nobody is pregnant for me." "She's just making that up right?" "Since your answering all the questions why are you asking me?" "I just know Lamar your not trying to be funny because I'm not laughing. "Why you took my phone and why did you answer it?" "I had nothing better to do while you were sleeping but to answer your phone and see who's calling you." "That's why you don't answer other people phone because you get what your not looking for." "What is that suppoose to mean that you mess with her?" "Tyra, I told you I don't mess with that lady." "Call her then and ask her why she's calling your phone." "I'm not calling her." "Well I guess that just let me know your dealing with her." "Alright Tyra if that's what you say. You gonna believe what you want anyway." "Right don't say nothing when I do it to you." "You're not stupid, you know better." "Men are really funny. How you figure you can do it to me and I'm suppose to just take it but when it's done back to you, you can't handle it." Lamar walked over to Tyra and looked her dead in her eyes and told her, "Don't you dare think about playing with me Tyra." "Yes, Lamar but I want you to know I'm not stupid." "If you say so my baby Lamar says kissing Tyra on her lips."

CHAPTER XVII

While Ron is on the park he gets a phone call. "Ron." "What Shannon? What do you want?" "I need to see you; I have something to tell you." "What is it that you can't tell me over the phone?" "Come pass by my house right quick." "Yeah alright, Shannon." Ron leaves the park to go by Shannon's house.

Ashley calls Lily. This is Lily speaking may I help you?" "Hey Lily you're just the girl I've been looking for." "I know it's all about me, Lily says. Come at me with your information because I know you have some." "That's right lady. First of all I went out last night after the aloha where it was women on women and men on men girl it was just wild. I was just standing there checking my surroundings thinking about going join in with the women." " So you thinking about going both ways I see." "Sometimes I do Lily you have a problem with that?" "No dear everybody is entitled to their own beliefs just don't dare play that shit over here." "Baby, I need somebody finer then you. You don't have enough meat on your bones for me and you don't meet my standards." "You damn skip it," Lily says smiling. "Are you really serious Ashley?" Lily asks wondering. "No, I'm just kidding. Anyway Lily I saw Nicollet in there. She came telling me that she and Ronald are still fucking with each other. She also wanted me to know that the girl Shannon he's fucking with to is supposed to be pregnant for him." "Really?" "Girl yes." "You don't think that whore is just saying that to be messy? Ashley sometimes girls do say things to be messy and you can't believe everything you hear but you never know. Time will tell." "Yes time will but I'm going to tell Dionne that girl don't deserve that," Ashley says.

Ron makes it over by Shannon house with an attitude. Ron rings the door bell. "Open the door I don't have all day Shannon." "Damn, Ron you don't have to beat the door down." "What did you ask me to come over here for?" "To tell you I'm pregnant with your child." "What?" "Your what pregnant?" Ron asked again like his ears were playing tricks on him. "What are you going to do with it?" Ron asks. "I'm going to keep my baby; I'm not going to have an abortion." "I don't know what you're going to do Shannon." "Ron what you thought was going to happen if your having sex without protection." "I have a family already." "Oh well, Ron you should have thought about that when you were all up in me." "Shannon you better go sit the fuck down somewhere." "Alright Ron you can leave now I told you what I had to tell you." Ron slammed the door behind him. What the fuck am I going to do Ron thought to hisself.

CHAPTER XVIII

When Will and Donald got back in town they drove straight to Brenda's house. "It's me big girl it's your man big Will." Brenda ran to the door with a big cookie smile on her face. "Hi, my man." "Come on B, let daddy put this big dick on you right quick. I have Donald in the car waiting on me. We're just getting back in town." "Why did you bring him with you if you knew you wasn't going to be able to stay long?" "Brenda baby quiet with all the questions pull your thongs to the side and bend over." Brenda did as she was told. Will pounded her over and over again. He didn't even give Brenda a chance to get hers but he instantly got his. "Thanks baby that was good," Will said as he was pulling his boxers up. "What Will? That's it? That's all I get?" "Brenda I told you Donald was waiting on me. I'll call you later. Maybe I'll pass back." Will left. Brenda sat on her couch asking herself, what is wrong with me? Is my self esteem low because of my size? Why am I allowing him to have me anytime he wants and that's far as it goes. Why God am I allowing this to happen to me. Lord, please help me to be a stronger woman in this situation, Brenda prayed.

Will got back in the car with Donald. "You have me out here head first like it's not damn near a hundred degrees." "I had to handle my business right quick." "So you went got your dick wet?" "Soaked that bitch pussy juicy and good. Donald laughs as he daps Will off. "You're a fool dude."

"Ronald what do you want to eat?" Dionne asks. "Anything you cook baby." "Go head and get Cache' ready for bed while I finish up with dinner." "Sure sweetie." "Ronald, I called you earlier to tell you something but you rushed me off the phone like you had so much going on." "No, it wasn't like that. I was on the park with Jeffery and the fellows we were kicking it." "Well I took a pregnancy test earlier and I'm pregnant." Ronald looked stunned as he thinks to himself. What the hell is going on? Two more damn babies. I can't handle anymore news. Ronald thought to hisself. "Are you ok?" Dionne ask Ron with suspicious because of the way Ron was looking when Dionne gave him the news. "Yes, I'm ok. You just caught me off guard." "I'm sorry; I just thought you should know." "I understand." Ron said rubbing his forehead with his guilty conscious coming on him. "Here Cache' come sit down and eat so you can get in the bed." "Alright mommy." "Ron you can turn the lights off when ya'll finish. I'm going to go lay down I don't feel good." "No problem Dionne go get your rest."

Lily is in the ticket line at the airport when she runs into Lamar. "What's up with you Lily?" Lamar asks. "I'm good, thanks." "How are you and Tyra?" Lamar grabs Lily around the waist with a smirk on his face. "Stop playing with me sexy." "Boy you think you have so much game. Coming at me with those weak ass lines, lines I don't fall for." "It's not like that Lily. It's not what you think." "Then Lamar tell me what it's like because I'm confused. When we first got together you told me you didn't have a girl and then all of a sudden now you have a girlfriend. That's funny to me real game you have." "Let me explain." "Wrong you don't owe me an explanation that's your situation and her problem. If you want you can hit me up I have a flight to catch." "Where are you going?" Lamar asks curious. "To Miami on the beaches so I can put on my two piece and think about sucking you. Syke,"

Lily says laughing. Lily remark made Lamar arouse. "Lily why did you tell that girl you were pregnant for me?" "Because you told me you were single remember. I really didn't what I said since you want play with my intelligence. "I'm going to give you a call baby." "Bye pookie with your fine self." Just the sight of Lamar made Lily hot. He is so handsome he should be my stripper Lily thought out loud boarding her flight. Lamar smiled with his bedroom eyes and walked off.

CHAPTER XIX

Several months have passed. Shannon is eight months pregnant and Dionne is seven months pregnant. Ron has been doing better. He stopped staying out for several nights. Lily and Lamar rectify their situation despite of Lamar's so called girlfriend. Sasha talks to Jeffery and Donald when she needs money. Ashley got pregnant for a boy named Derrick and their not together anymore.

Ron runs in the house. He dropped Dionne off a bag of money. "Here bay this for you. I'll hit you up later." "Alright Ron I'm leaving to go out of town and Cache' is by your mom." "I'll pick her up later. Have a safe trip." "Come on Ashley lets go." "That man stays on the go day and night huh?" "I'm tired of living like this." "I know what you mean Dionne." I can't talk Dionne my crazy ass went and got pregnant for a bum that gave me Chlamydia and he still sleeping around. That is so embarrassing. I don't know what I was thinking." "Ashley you can't trust none of them they are all idiots and need to grow up and think about the importance of life." "Now Dionne there's some good men out there I must say. We just choose the wrong ones." "Maybe your right Ashley." "While we're on this conversation Dionne I have something to tell you. I'm coming at you as a friend and please don't tell who told you." "I won't tell who told Ashley what is it?" "I heard that some girl named Shannon is supposed to be pregnant for Ron." "Really?" Dionne said upset. "Yes Dionne and she's suppose to go in before you." "What?" Dionne says annoyed. Dionne was so steamed it felt like fire was burning from her feet to her head and she needed water to put it out. "Are you okay Dionne?" "No, I'm not. I feel like killing that low down dirty bitch. "It probably was that hoe that was looking at me crazy at Will's party." "Probably girl you know how stupid they look when they wish they were the wifey instead of the side bitch." "I can't wait until this three day vacation is over so I can confront Mr. Ronald Brown." "Just don't kill him Dionne." "That bastard not even worth it."

"Sasha what time are you going to be ready so I can knock off over here and send my workers home?" Donald asked. "I'll be ready in about an hour or two." "I need to know a definite time lady." "Okay about four." "I'll be there around four-thirty." Sasha hung up the phone. "Man what am I going to do with these cats?" Sasha looks in the mirror and smiles at herself. Sasha had a light brown complexion, long silky hair with curves in all the right places. You couldn't tell Sasha she didn't have it going on. That's right spend, spend, spend your money on me Sasha says to herself out loud. Buy me Versace, Gucci, Louie, Tiffany and Company in order for me to give you "Pam" (pussy, ass and mouth)." Sasha starts laughing. Yeah right if that's what they think.

"Akira what movie do you want to see?" Will asks. "The one with the aliens?" Before Will could ask for two tickets to the alien movie the boy at the ticket booth hands Will two tickets commented that was the last two tickets for the 8:15 show. "Do you want anything to eat popcorn, hotdogs or something?" "Nachos and cheese." After getting their food Will goes to the restroom while Akira goes into the movie to find their seat. "Well look who's here Mr. William Sams." Will looks up and sees Brenda. "Hey baby." "Will don't baby me." "What's the attitude for Brenda?" "I'm tired of every time we're together you always have to run off." "I be having business to take care of." "Will I don't think we need to deal with each other. Who are you here with?" "My people." "Your people huh? Where's your people when you're all up in me?" "I guess at home. I don't know I'm not her keeper." "Let me go William because I would hate for your people as you put it to come see you out here talking to me and she bust the piss out cha." "She knows better. Believe that." "Your ass is mighty cheeky. You want to do your thing with no questions asked." "See how smart you are?" Will says smacking Brenda on her ass. Brenda looks back at Will, "You like that don't you?" "You know I do "B."

CHAPTER XX

Dionne returns back home from Miami. She walks in the house. No sound of Ron. Dionne calls his phone over and over again. No answer. Where could he be? He's not home and he's not answering his phone. Where does he have my baby? Thirty minuets later Ron and Cache' comes walking through the door. Cache run up to Dionne saying, "Hey mom I'm so happy your home." "I'm happy to be home Cache', home with you." "Mom dad bought me by Nicollet." Ron turned around in shock looking at Cache'. "What? Your dad bought you where?" "By Nicollet where my brother live." Dionne swung around like an evil witch. "What the hell you doing bringing my baby by Nicollet?" Dionne screams. "That child don't know what's she's talking about." "So now you trying to say Cache' is crazy. A five year old doesn't know who she sees." "Alright, I bought her over there so Nicollet could give her a bath." "Why the hell your tired ass couldn't bathe her? I don't need any of your bitches to give me a hand in nothing when it comes down to my child. Don't you ever bring my child around her again. Don't think I don't know your fucking her behind my back." "What are you talking about Dionne?" "I know your confused right? Eventually you'll get it." Ron is standing in the kitchen looking puzzled. "Another thing mister; who is Shannon? Is she suppose to be pregnant for you?" "Where did you get that from? You believe anything somebody tells you." "Whatever, I'm about to find out if she is or not? "How?" Ron asked mysteriously. "I have her number and I would like to know what she has to say." "Alright, call her then." Dionne dialed Shannon on speaker phone.

"Can I speak with Shannon?" "Speaking, who's this?" "This is Dionne." "Do I know you Dionne?" Shannon asked sarcastically? "This is Ronald's girlfriend, baby momma which ever one you want me to be." "What? Why are you calling my phone?" "I want to know are you pregnant for Ron?" "Ask him he needs to tell you." "Bitch you not pregnant for me you lying whore," Ron screams aggravated. "Ron I'm not going to argue with you we know the deal." "Fuck you bitch that's not my fucking baby. That bitch is a liar," Ron said trying to convince Dionne. "Whatever Ron time will tell a baby can't stay a secret" and Shannon hangs up her phone. "So you believe her Dionne?" "I don't know what to believe to tell you the truth." "Well fuck it Dionne believe what you want. Those hoes don't want us together anyway."

"Donald shit you don't have to blow the horn like that. I heard it the first time." "My bad baby." "Just drive me to the mall alright pimping. Turn my song up." Sasha started singing. "Lic, lic, lick it like a lollipop. I said he's so sweet I wanna lick the rapper." Donald looks at Sasha with a strange look. "Problem?" Sasha asks. "No I'm just looking at how pretty your lips are." "You better just look cause they won't be touching you." "Yeah, I know. Come on so we can get in this mall and get out." "Don't be rushing me Donald." Sasha had Donald spending his money on her in Saks Fifth Avenue, Coach, Steve Madden and Victoria's Secret. "Alright, Donald lets go. I got all I came for." "Good now let's go get a room." "A room," Sasha says in disgust. My cycle is down I can't do nothing today." "I bet Sasha with your game running you know what

I'll just keep that comment to myself, Donald says mad as hell. "I'm serious." "Well let me drop your ass off home." In the back of Sasha's mind she thought that was a good lie she used.

CHAPTER XXI

Two months pass and Shannon delivers her baby. Jeffery calls Ronald to inform him about Shannon. "Say bra ya girl Shannon had her baby." "She did?" Ron asked. "Yeah man she still in the hospital on the 5th floor." "Alright I'm going to go up there to see her." Ron gets up, gets dressed, and leaves out the house to go to the hospital. When Ron made it to the hospital, Shannon was sitting on the edge of the bed feeding the baby. "What's up?" Ron asks when he walked in the room. "Look who's here Hilton your dad the one who cursed us out a couple months ago trying to prove a point to his woman." "Let me see her," Ron says not even paying attention to what Shannon was saying. "How did you feel doing that, like a man?" "No. I did that so she could shut up with that craziness." "So what you're going to deny my baby to her so she don't put you out." "She can't put me out no where I pay all the bills." "Mighty funny, you lied about my baby." "Shannon shut up with that shit. I have enough on my mind." Ron's phone rings. "This is Dionne so don't say nothing," Ron waved at Shannon saying. "I want daddy," Shannon whispers. "Hello." "Hey where are you?" "Taking care of business, why what's up." "I need you to pick Cache' up from by my mother. I also wanted you to know my doctor says tomorrow she is inducing my labor so we need to get the room ready for the baby." "Alright fat I'll go get our daughter. I'll see you when I get home." Ron hangs up his phone and Shannon grabs Hilton out Ron's arm. "Go head and pick up your daughter and go home so you can get ready for your son's arrival," Shannon says with jealousy. "It's not like that Shannon." "Whatever Ron just go." Ron kissed the baby on her hand and leaves the hospital.

Nicollet is on the phone with her girlfriend cracking up laughing. "Child you know Shannon had a baby girl for Ron and Dionne's in the hospital right now about to have her baby. The funny part is I heard Ron called and cursed Shannon out while Dionne was standing there saying the baby wasn't his yet he ran to the hospital when the baby was born." "That's a shame Nicollet; both of them are stupid for Ronald that makes no sense. Men wonder why women cheat. If men could stop acting like one woman is not good enough for them and stop getting busted when they mess around with other women then maybe we wouldn't have to go out to find someone to make us happy." "Isn't that the truth girl?" "I wouldn't let him play me like that. When he came to me and told me he wanted Dionne it hurted. I sat down and thought it's a reason for this and now I see Karma came back on her twice as bad. I'm just glad he's not my man no more I just have him when I want to. Let Dionne put up with those problems." "I know that's real let her deal with it."

Kimora, Ron and his friends were at the hospital when Dionne had her baby. They were all acknowledging how much he looks like his dad. "Come on Ron sign these papers so the baby can have your last name. Dionne's says exhausted. Sign right there on the dotted line." "Ronald Darrel Brown Jr." Ron says happy. "Let's go get the room together for when they come home tomorrow Kimora sighs to Ron as she picks up her purse. "Right, let's go. I'll call you later bay." "Alright, Dionne says as she rolled over to go back to sleep."

"Yes, that feels so good." Lily screams while Lamar is sexing her. Lily was sucking and blowing on Lamar's neck and in his ear as she was on top of him. "Yeah Lily sex me like that, Lamar tells Lily as she was riding him on her toes. Girl I never ran into nobody that could handle me like this I'm use to being in control. You're a beast." Lily smiles as she moves up and down "Your dealing with a woman." "I'm about to shoot off," Lamar says loud as he enjected. Lily took a deep breathe. "Now you go tell Tyra, as long as she's fucking you I'll be fucking you. Just as well as it's her dick it's mine too. I want her to know this is a sharing and caring world." "Shut up girl with your crazy self." "You think that's funny," Lamar sighs as he was wiping himself. "No honey you do she loves you not me. You're the one hurting her not me so don't try to blame me." "Go to sleep Lily, goodnight."

Chapter XXII

Dionne made it home from the hospital. Ron started staying out again. He would catch his attitudes when Dionne would ask him questions. Ron would fight Dionne for questioning him or when he's mad about situations in the street. He would pick a fight so Dionne would get mad and she would tell him to leave. Then Ron would go out and be with his other women. People would call Dionne telling her that Ron was seen in his car with other women. Ron would beat Dionne over and over again. The truth was what Ron was scared to admit. One day he chocked Dionne and her eyes rolled to the back of her head he thought for a moment he killed her because she stopped breathing. Poor Cache' would go to school shaking because of everything she was seeing with her parents. She started felling test at school. Counselors stepped in to try to get answers but Cache' would never tell what was going on at home.

"Kimora please come over here please. I need a friend to talk to. I feel like I'm losing my mind. I'm breaking down like nobody loves me not even God." "Dionne hold yourself together. I'm on my way. I just need to drop off my kids and I'll be right there. I won't be long at all." Dionne hung up the phone crying uncontrollable after just fighting with Ron. He left her there all bruised up.

"Damn man what's wrong with you breathing all hard and all scratched up." "Man I just had to handle up on Dionne." "For what?" Donald asks. "I'm sick of her ass questioning me about Shannon and the baby and always nagging me about this and that. She is working on my nervous about Nicollet and my son. I'm just tired of all the bullshit." "Come on Ron lets go get a drink and talk," Donald suggested. "You need to calm your nerves."

Akira and Will are going out to dinner at the same restaurant where Sasha and Lily are having dinner. Akira walks in front of Will strutting like nobody else has nothing on her as the hostess was directing them to their table. When Sasha looked up and notices Akira strutting hard with her short dress and stilettos, she almost chocked off her steak. "Lily what is that?" Sasha smirks as she looks at Akira. "That's the girl from Will's party. She's the one they say is his main woman the one who Brenda was fussing with." "Girl, you're kidding right, yeah I do recognize her? "I have something on me Will?" Akira asks when she notices Sasha and Lily looking her up and down. "No you don't why?" "These things are looking at me like their crazy." "Oh no she didn't," Lily says standing up walking towards Akira. Will grabs Akira and moves her to his right side away from Lily and Sasha table. "That's what you better do Will is get her before I post mark her ass. By the way you do have something on you a pound of damn make up." "Hating is a sickness go get well lil girls!" Akira says laughing. "Keep talking I'm going wear you out in here." Sasha grabs Lily. "Lily she is not even worth it. Let's finish our dinner." "Let's go sit down Akira all of this is not cause for." "That's right," the waitress says standing looking at all the commotion. "She got the right one acting like she's all that. Brenda is crazy I would have been tagged her." "She lets Will play her as his fuck toy." "Your right about that besides this track head trick doesn't have nothing on Brenda. Will is all up in her face like she's all that." "Those women of course are only with him just for his money." "Baby please, Will is a handsome looking man." "If you think so Sasha. I mean everyone is entitled to their own opinion. Let's leave the waitress a tip. Let Will go ahead and entertain his main chick." They both starts laughing.

When Kimora made it to Dionne's house she was sitting on the floor in front of the bed rocking hugging Lil Ronald and Cache'. "Hi baby how are you doing?" Kimora asked Dionne sadly. "I'm not doing to good Kimora; I'm broken and hurt on the inside. I can't take it anymore." "Tee, Tee," Cache' calls out to Kimora. "Yes sweetie," Kimora answers. "I feel sad when I see my mom and dad fight. It really scares me." Dionne starts crying harder. "I know it scares you." Kimora says as she rubs Cache' on her back. "Dionne why don't you leave?" Why don't you get out of this abusive relationship?" "Kimora, that's easier said than done. I love him too much. I love him more than anything." "So you mean to tell me you love him more than you love your kids? You love him more than you love yourself? You're going to continue on going through this emotional and physical abuse because you love so much?" Dionne didn't respond. "You know like I know Dionne you better get up and get yourself together. Next Sunday we're going to church because something has to give. Dionne you have to pray and ask God to keep you covered because Ron can seriously hurt you. Ask God to give you strength to leave this ungodly relationship." "I will Kimora and thanks for coming by. I'll give you a call later." "Anytime friend I mean it anytime you need me I'm here for you."

"Why isn't he answering his phone anything could be wrong," Dionne said frustrated. "I am so fed up with this boy; I don't know what to do." "Ron answer your phone," Nicollet suggest while Ron is pounding her. "That's Dionne keep calling my phone." "Well answer the phone and see what she wants so she can stop calling on my time." "I'll see her when I get home. I'm gone hear her mouth when I get there anyway." "Whatever that's on you don't say I didn't warn you."

Ron came walking in the house at four in the morning. Dionne wakes up out of her sleep. "Where the hell have you been? I've been calling your phone all night and you didn't answer. Anything could've been wrong." "Dionne I swear I don't want to hear this shit." "I guess you don't since your just coming in from your bitch house." "How do you know that?" Ron asks. "I'm not stupid that's how. Can you tell me Mr. Brown what else could you be doing at four in the morning? I would love to mention the fact that I'm not having sex with you so where you getting it from?" "I'm not getting it from anywhere smart ass." "Yeah right Ron, I bet your not." "Go to sleep Dionne before you wake up the children." "Now you're concerned about the children you bastard how nice is that." "Good night," Ron says as he turned over to go to sleep. Fuss with yourself because I'm tired."

CHAPTER XXIII

"Push Ashley, push a little harder. Here it comes. It's a girl," the doctor tells Ashley as she cut the navel cord. "She is beautiful," the doctor says as she hands Ashley her baby. "She is beautiful," Ashley says with the feeling of happiness and some deep down hurt. To know that the father of her daughter wasn't concerned whether the baby was born or not gave Ashley thoughts that came in full force. "Do you want me to call the baby's father in?" The doctor asks Ashley. "That's not a good idea, he's not here. Actually, he was just a sperm donor. Everything was good between us until I got pregnant and then he just went about his business saying the baby wasn't his. He couldn't stand up to his responsibility." "I'm sorry to hear that." "He says I tried to trap him by getting pregnant. I should have been wiser with my choice. My daughter and I will be just fine without him." "You will be just fine just keep your head up," Dr. Johnson says while hugging her patient.

"Dionne please hurry up before we're late for church." "I'm coming right now Kimora." Dionne gets in the car. "Sister, I like to make it to church on time for praise and worship. It gets me in the spirit. We lift God up in prayer for his goodness." "I understand. I'm sorry." "Dionne that's fine. I just wanted you to know for next time pookie."

"Praise the Lord everyone," the preacher shouts as he walks to the pulpit. "Some of us have to separate ourselves from some people in order to receive our blessings from God. God is too good to be surrounding ourselves around negative people. It will block your blessing. I'd rather stand alone because I know my father will take care of me. He will bring me through all my trails and tribulations. There's nothing I go through that

God will not bring me out of. He says all you need is to have faith the size of a mustard seed." "Preach pastor," the congregation shouts. "If nobody loves me I know God does. He's a good God and a forgiven God. Just go to him in prayer and give him all your problems. Know that the battle is not yours it's the Lord's. He is the only one that can handle it better than you can. Is there anyone that needs a church home or somebody to pray for them? Come on up to the alter." People were coming from everywhere going up to the alter. Dionne gets out of her seat overwhelmed. She was bent over crying so hard. She had other people in the congregation crying as well. It's like they felt all her pain. Dionne felt a lot better when the elder was rubbing her on her back repeatedly saying that everything is going to be alright. Just bring it to God in prayer.

"Dionne how did you enjoy church?" Kimora asked. I really enjoyed it girl I feel so much better. Things are about to change in my household and I mean that. It's time for a change within me and my house and for my kids. Ron is going to have to do better or he has to go. I am not taking anymore abuse from him. I will be bringing all my problems to the mighty father above. I have to love myself more than I love Ron. I know I deserve more and better than what he's been giving me. I have my mind made up. This is truly my final straw dealing with all that comes with Ron." "That's right friend, yourself first. That's the first step in getting yourself together. I'm happy for you."

Ashley is home with her new baby with all her friends at her house to help. "She is to pretty," Lily says while Lamar is standing over her shoulder. "Unfortunately your genes are not strong enough to make a beautiful baby like this," Lamar grins while he kisses the baby on the hand. "Can you back up off me and give me and the baby some breathing room. You acting like this your baby," Lily says to Lamar laughing. "I'm just making sure you don't play games with me because I don't want no children," Lamar says joking. You should be happy someone wants to stand this close to you with your dog breath ass." "Real funny Lamar," Lily says with a serious look. "Did you talk to that deadbeat dad of hers?" Sasha asks Ashley. "Yes, I did." "What did he have to say?" "The same thing he said when I first told him I was pregnant. Talking about he can't believe me. Going on and on about how I was not suppose to get pregnant and have no baby because he has his family to take care of. His mom and sister not even claming my baby and it's sad because my baby looks just like them people." "Forget his tired ass and his family. You and the baby don't need them." "We really don't but I bet I won't make this mistake again." "Ashley your baby is not a mistake. She is a gift a blessing from God." "Next time I'll be married and stable and my next baby will be for my husband." "That's right," Donald says. "Oh you shut the hell up," Lily screams. Everyone starts laughing.

"Come on Cache' baby it's time to get in the bed." "Yes mommy." Dionne covers Cache' up and kisses her on her forehead as she finished reading her book. "Goodnight baby, I love you." "I love you too. Mommy, I don't want you and daddy to fight anymore?" Dionne stood in door to Cache's room holding back her tears. "No honey, we're not going to fight anymore." 'Thanks, mommy." Dionne went in her room and got on her knees to pray. "Dear God this is your child Dionne coming to you and begging you to teach me how to love myself way more than I love man. I want to love you more than anything. Make my weak body strong. God draw me closer to you. I want my steps to be ordered by you. God my self-respect and self-esteem is so low Lord, please help me to build it back up. Please fix my broken heart. Every time I look in the mirror my reflection is someone ugly because I allowed man to destroy me. God I'm not perfect, but with you I can become a better person. When I cry, allow the tears that fall down my face to be tears of joy and not tears of hurt. I'm now giving you all my burdens. God last of all please help Ron to become a better man. God I'm giving it all to you right now. I know you can handle it better than me. I trust you more with it than myself. Take control of my situation. I love you Lord and thank you for allowing me to come to you in prayer. Amen."

CHAPTER XXIV

"What's up Lamar?" Donald asks. "Nothing at all just leaving from by Tyra. I was on my way by Lily. Why? What's up?" "I was just hitting you up to invite you over to my house. Me and the fellas are over here drinking and playing cards." "Cool Donald, I'll be over there when I leave from by Lily." "My boy you're really digging Lily huh?" "She's cool, crazy too. She tells you what's on her mind and don't care who don't like it." "You are so right about that. I knew she was crazy when she told Tyra how I didn't tell her I had a girlfriend." "She told Tyra that Lamar?" "She sure did and didn't give a damn how Tyra felt." "That's good for your ass; you should have told Lily you had an ole lady." "Yeah, I know I should have told her, but Lily said I'm for her and Tyra." "Man Lily is wild she really don't give a damn." "I'll be there in about thirty minutes I'm pulling up by crazy right now." "Alright, I'll see you then."

Donald hangs up the phone with Lamar and walks in his huge living room where the rest of the fellas were. His living room is decorated with paintings on the wall of African art. The art hangs on the wall with warm colors. He has statues in three corners, and a deep brown micro fiber living room set. When you look up you see a sixty two inch flat screen television that hangs on the wall. To the right stands a bar that has all types of drinks. Ron walks up to the radio to turn it up louder rapping out loud. "You can have whatever you like. I want your body; I need your body..." "Man you a fool," Will yells over the music to Ron. Will gets a cigar out and lights it as he sits back on the couch and crosses his legs. "Well fellas we're about to have an Oprah show going on in here. No I mean a Dr.

Phil show and I am going to be Dr. Phil asking ya'll the questions." "Questions about what," Donald asks curious. "What is it going to be about?" Lamar says walking in the door. "What's up peps?" Donald says dapping Lamar off. "Nothing trying to see what our Dr. Phil show is going to be about?" "I thought I'll never get it out with Donald rude as interrupting me," Will blurted. "Alright the subject is "Why do men Cheat." "Yeah that's an interesting subject." Ron says all happy. "I knew you would like that. Mr. Ron let's start with you." First question, your wife is home everyday being faithful to you, taking care of your kids and she has your dinner ready for you when you get home. With all that being said, why do you still cheat on her?" "First off dude, I know when I was in jail Dionne was dealing with somebody else." "How do you know if that was true? Did that man you say she was dealing with, ever discuss that with you. Did he tell you he was dealing with her." "No, but other people told me." "I'm not interested in what people told you. I'm not saying it's not true but even if it was that's when you were in jail. If you suspected her messing around, why did you come out to still be with her?" "She held it down for me and she kept it one-hundred." "That's what should matter and nothing else." "Yes, it does matter because she should have never fucked anybody while I was down." "So what you're doing it to her makes you feel better?" "No, it just really fucked me up when I heard that." "So that's what made you go make a baby on her and sleep with other women? To make the situation worse your still sleeping with your baby momma Nicollet and you left her to be with Dionne." "Right, right," Ron responds.

"Do you enjoy doing it?" "No I don't I was playing catch back." "So do you feel better since you've played catch back?" "No once again, I really don't. I made a baby and I regret doing that because Cache' and Lil Ron mean a lot to me, and if Dionne ever finds out about that baby she will go crazy." "Alright Donald your turn." "I'm ready peeps." "Why do you think you have to cheat on women?" "Well Dr. Phil I mean Dr. Will; let me put it to you like this. I'm not committing myself to no one. The reason why I deal with several women because I like the different sizes they come in." "What sizes is that sir?" "Big hips, nice size booty, big thighs and a size D bra. I also like them when they wear their sexy clothes and the ones that have the small waist line with nice tits that sit up like they went got a breast injection or whatever they get." The fella's started laughing saying "boy you need to control yourself." Last but not least Dr. Will when they have their nice fitting jeans on and doing their sexy walk it makes my dick rise!" "Now you Mr. Lamar same question." "I like a woman that has fire stuff. My girl shit so fire there's nobody I've ever been with feels like her or can handle me like she can. Another reason why I cheat is because the different feelings of different pussy. I really like the ones that stay wet. The other night I went out, I got fucked up and passed out, so my girl got to my phone; Lily happens to call. I never told Lily I had a girlfriend. I cheated on Tyra because I wanted to try some new pussy. After being with Lily, I couldn't let that juicy stuff go. I kept that girlfriend information to myself. One thing about Lily, she is the only person that can work that thing backwards. So I know I'm not leaving her alone any time soon." "So you're making the calls?" Will ask Lamar. "You just sit back and watch Dr. Will. Understand Dr. Will she's not running out either. I put my work in." "Your turn now Will," all the fellas said. "Why do you cheat?" "The women don't want to stay off me because of who I am. I can't take a nagging ass woman when she starts nagging I'm off to the next one that's not making all that noise in my ear. Pass me some peanuts and a beer," Will say's to Donald. "Would any of ya'll get married?" "Maybe one day," Ronald replies. "I really don't know," Donald says. It depends."

"Well I'm feeling good right now so I'm going home to Dionne and the kids and handle my business with my girl." "Go head with your crazy ass and don't be tripping on that girl tonight," Donald yells as Ronald was leaving out the door. "I'm not I'm chilling tonight". "While you leaving out the door Ron, everyone else leaving too." "Donald you putting everybody out like your having company over and your the one asked me to come over here," Lamar argues. Before Lamar could finish a nice dressed lady walks up to the door smelling so damn good with a pair high shorts on and a short shirt with her belly ring showing. "How ya'll doing?" The lady says as she greets them. "We're good," everyone said as they were leaving. "See you later Donald everything was nice."

Ron made it home. He got in the bed with Dionne kissing her and rubbing her down. "Hey bay," Ron whispers. "Hi, Ron where are you coming from?" "I was by Will with the rest of the gang. Just having a drinks talking and listening to the radio." "Oh I got you." Ron continued to rub Dionne down and tried to stick his finger in her but Dionne moved his hand showing no interest. "What is wrong with you, why you moving my hand? "Ron it's just not okay for you to come trying to have sex with me after you beat me cursed me out, stay out till the next day and you always getting mad every time I question you." "Look you're my woman; you're supposed to satisfy me whenever I want you to." "If I don't Ron?" Dionne quickly question. If you don't you want somebody else will satisfy me?" "That's if you want someone else to satisfy you. I can't stop you from doing what you're going to do anyway." "Alright Dionne, fuck it then." "It's something, how you feel you can do me what you want and then act like nothing is wrong." "Dionne stop talking to me because your pissing me off." "I know I am Ron. That's because things are not going Ronald's way, oh well."

CHAPTER XXV

Its Christmas time and everyone is looking for gifts especially Ron's baby mommas. Nicollet calls Ronald's phone. Ronald answers, "Yeah what do you want Nicollet?" "I know my damn son is looking forward to having his toys on Christmas day." "Look, I don't need you calling my phone telling me the same damn thing like I'm stupid." "I bet you're not telling Dionne that. I bet her children have their toys." "That's ya'll problem ya'll worry about Dionne to much instead of worrying about yourself." "If you say so you just better have what I called you for." "Yeah alright, disgusting ass girl I'm going to drop off his toys, and don't call my phone no more once he gets them," Ron screams as he hangs up in Nicollet ear. Ron thinks to himself damn baby mommas work on my nerves the biggest mistake I made is having all these baby mommas.

"Mr. Lamar I would like panties and lingeric from Victoria's secret and you can stop at Mac and get me the new colors they have out." "For what Lily so you can scribble it all over face trying to give yourself a face lift." "No sucker you need to get a tattoo on your black ass face." "You're jealous of me." "Buster you sound like you look 'stupid'." "What you asking me to buy you that for anyway?" "So I can wear for your tired ass." "I don't want you to wear nothing for me with your big cheesy ass." "I know I'm cheesy and you loving it." "You know what I love about you?" Lamar asks looking at Lily. "Don't play with me Lamar," Lily says while playfully punching Lamar in his back. "I'm just playing baby. I'm gone treat you right as long as you treat me right." "I will Lamar you my baby. I'm gone get you a manikin with some Santa Clause lingerie." Lamar and Lily start laughing and hugging each other. "Oh," Lily says, I'm going to put a bug in Tyra's ear letting her know I'm still fucking our man. That's going to be her Christmas gift from me." "Don't do that," Lamar says smiling. "I'll think about it, it depends on how I feel at that time. Now come on drop me off so I can meet Sasha so we can go shopping."

"Ron are you going to bring Cache' to school this morning?" "Why do I have to bring her? I have something to do." "So what you have some running to do? Why you can't drop her off before you start all you're running, while I drop our son off." "Dionne you sure work on my damn nerves. I guess I'll bring her. Come on Cache' lets go. Kiss your mom and your brother bye." "Love you brother and you to Mom." "We love you to Cache'." Ron and Cache' walks out the house. Dionne hurries and grabs Lil Ron and her coat running to the truck. Alright he's not too far. I'm right behind him. Dionne turns her radio on and pops in her CD, playing "Bust the windows out your car." After five whole years of your bullshit Dionne was singing. That's right Jasmine sing that song. Right turn, left turn, straight down after the four way stop sign; he pulls to the left side. Ron and Cache' get out the car and they begin to walk into the school. I'm going to stay parked right here by this tree so he won't see me when he walk's out the building from bringing Cache' to her class, Dionne thought to herself. Ron walks back out the building on his phone and hops back into his car. He drives off and makes two left turns stops at the stop sign and makes another left turn. He goes further down right turn then left turn and he pulls to the left side and parks his car under the carport in which to Dionne was an unfamiliar house. As Dionne sits at the corner parked she watches as he got out the car and rings the doorbell. A lady comes to the door with a robe on and a rag tied around her head. Ron walks in and closes the door behind him.

I wonder who she is. Dionne thought. Dionne picked up her phone and dials Ron number. After five rings she hung up the phone and dials again. No answer Dionne called him back to back and he finally answers. Ron yells, "Hello" as if Dionne was disturbing him. "Did you get Cache' to school in time?" "Yes I did." "That's good what are you doing?" "Nothing much just handling a little business right now." "Must be nice I hear you Ron." "I thought I saw a car just like yours on a street. I forgot the name of the street." "I don't think that was my car Dionne." "Maybe if you look out the window it might just be yours." Ron begins to wonder what the hell Dionne is talking about. Shannon was sitting on the bed looking at Ron like she wishes he would hurry the hell up off the phone. "What the hell do you mean Dionne?" "Look out the window. Look out the window and see if that's your car under the carport." Ron pulled one blind down and his mouth dropped wide open when he saw Dionne outside in her truck. He hurried up and turned from the window. "I already know you're in there so you might as well come out." "Alright," Ron said quickly trying to get a lie together. "What's wrong with you?" Shannon screams when she sees Ron walk from the window. "How the fuck did Dionne find out where you stay?" "I don't know. How you expect me to know that?"

Ron walks outside and Dionne steps out her car. Ron's whole body was nervous; he was looking like he saw a ghost. "You're taking care of business huh?" "Yeah bay, just a lil something." "I feel you sir," Dionne replies. I was just wondering who is the lady that opened the door for you when you first got here?" How the hell did she see all that Ron thought to himself? "That's one of my boys' sisters." "I respect you getting your thoughts together real quick. Tell me why you're stuttering?" "I'm not stuttering Dionne." "Let me meet him because I must have never met him before." "He's not here yet that's who I'm waiting on," Ron says nervously. "You know Ron I would really like to meet his sister." "She's lying down and I'm not about to go get her up. You really need to leave Dionne." "You right I do need to leave. I'm not until I meet your boys' sister. Are you going to walk me to the door or do I need to go to the door myself?" Ron just stood there like a stiff solider. Dionne walks up to the door and rings the doorbell. "Who is it?" Shannon said looking out the blinds. "It's Dionne, Ron girlfriend better yet his fiancé." Shannon opens the door with her hands on her hips and a boot in her mouth. "May I help you?" Shannon says with an attitude. "I just wanted to come say hi and introduce myself since Ron is here waiting on his boy." Ron was trying to get Shannon's attention so she would not go along with Dionne's suspension. "His boy, his boy," Shannon repeats. For future reference his boy is his daughter he's over here seeing. You know the one he never admitted he had." "Are you serious?" "Yes I am." "Yes he did deny the child," Dionne says. "I know he did to you he knew it was his child when he came to the hospital to see us." "The hospital Ron what the hell is she talking about?" "She is lying Dionne; I don't even know why you're entertaining that miserable bitch." "Miserable bitch huh? Dionne my baby is 11 months and Ron is here twice a week visiting her." "Yeah right," Ron says pissed off. "Ronald for real tell me the truth is it your baby?" "No that's not my fucking baby and you need to stop telling people that's my baby." Ronald says with anger in his voice. "Dionne you have to know this is his baby. What other reason would he be coming over here?" "Come on Dionne baby enough of this bullshit," Ron suggested. Dionne just felt so weak that she just wanted to scream. Her eyes were filled with tears to the point she could have cried herself a river. It felt like her heart broke into a thousand pieces because of the embarrassment. With all of the other stuff that Ron has done to her, her pride would not allow her to break down. "Thanks for the information Shannon." Dionne turns around and looks at Ron with hate in her heart. Dionne walks to her truck and pulls out a crow bar and runs up to Ron car and bust all four of Ron's windows out. "You are an embarrassment to me," Dionne was shouting. "What the hell are you doing Dionne? Have you lost your mind?" "Yes, I have lost my mind being with your no good ass this long. Ron I don't know what you're going to do but you need to come get your clothes out of my house today." Shannon was standing in her door laughing at Ron. "Bitch, you need to get your messy ass inside?" "How am I messy when you lied about my daughter? I wasn't denying my child for you and nobody else." "You better do something because it's a wrap on this." "Fuck you Ron," Shannon shouts out the door. "Yeah ok we'll see about that." Ron turns to Dionne mad as hell because of his windows. "Dionne what do you mean come get my clothes?" "Simple get you some bags and get your shit." "I pay all the bills I'm not going anywhere." "After tomorrow you don't have to worry about paying another bill. I trust in God and he will make a way out of no way all I have to have is faith the size of a mustard seed." "Yeah ok trust in your God." "I will Dionne says as she skeeted off. Looking in the back seat Dionne notices Lil Ronald waking up. "Hey baby momma is going to stop and give you a bottle then we're going home."

Dionne was so hurt as she was driving home. Tears begin to roll down her face uncontrollable. I will not go back. I am moving forward. Dionne called Kimora. Kimora answers her phone. "Hey girl what's up?" Can you believe that Ron got busted today by the girl that everybody was saying he had a baby for him. Can you believe he kept denying it to me over and over again every time I would ask him." "Yes, I do remember you telling me about that." "Child it was a mess. I felt so played. I bust him at the girl house and he still denies the child. Girl I don't know what's wrong with him, but he really needs help." "That's okay Dionne; just remember once you take your first step God will take care of the rest. Let God deal with him." "Well Kimora I'm going to call you back because I'm pulling up to the house. I told him to come get his clothes out of my house today." "Call me if you need me girl." "I will Kimora."

All the guys at the barber shop talking about Ron, Dionne and Shannon's early morning incident. "How did he let his guards down and didn't see Dionne following him?" Kahlil says. "I don't know but I know Dionne told him to get his shit and get out. I know he is so sick," Donald says. "I bet when he thinks about what he did he's going to realize those tramps weren't even worth it. You don't realize you have something good until it's gone." "I don't know what he's going to do," Will sighs. "I wish the best for my boy," Lamar says.

CHAPTER XXVI

Ron walks in the door with Cache' bringing her backpack inside. Dionne looked up at him and shook her head in disgrace. "Hi mommy, Cache' says running up kissing her mom on the jaw. "Hey pookie how was your day at school?" "It was good mommy, thanks for asking. Can you fix me a sandwich please?" "Sure. Cache' go to your room and I'll bring it to you." "Ok, mommy," Cache' says running to her room. Dionne looked up at Ronald and told him, "You have twenty minutes to have your stuff packed and out my house." "Dionne please. I'm not going anywhere." "Do you want to bet?" "Yep, bet your life on it," Ron replies. "Let me get my daughter together. I'll deal with you shortly. Here Cache' eat your sandwich and chips and drink your juice." "Yes mom," Cache' says. Dionne walks in the room back by Ron. "Now I'm not playing with you. You need to pack your stuff and go head by one of your other baby mommas. I'm telling you Ron, I'm not playing with you. I'm not the one for this with you today." "I pay the damn bills here so I'm not going anywhere." "See that's where I messed up at letting you pay all the bills so now you think you're entitled to live here no matter what you do to me but not anymore. I'm going to be alright and my bills will get paid. I'm not depending on you anymore to pay them." "Keep talking all that shit Dionne." "No Ron I'm finish wiping my ass with all your shit. "I want you out of my house now!" Dionne yells. "You won't be doing your dirt living here any longer." "Bitch I'm not going nowhere I said." "That's another reason I don't want you. I'm sick of all the emotional and physical abuse. That's the last bitch your going to call me." "Stop talking stupid then and you won't get cursed out." "For the last time I want your ass out my house. I don't have nothing for you here but your children and you can come visit them. The feelings are gone. So go head now you free to go do whatever you want to do and you don't have to sneak around anymore." "I don't want anybody else Dionne." "Are you serious Ronald? I wasn't enough for you before. I asked you to get out; you wanted to deal with all these women so now you go be with them?" "I'm sorry Dionne." "Please Ron the same ole repeated apologies are played out you just need to go ahead and go." Ron got so steamed up; he grabbed Dionne by the neck and threw her on the bed. "Didn't I tell you I'm not going anywhere," Ron says chocking Dionne. Dionne started crying, saying stop choking me as she gasped for air. "Your cheeky you want to cheat on me and expect for me to accept it." "Shut the fuck up," Ron says pulling Dionne's hair. "Leave Ron, just please go and leave me alone." Cache' ran in the room screaming to the top of her lungs. She heard the commotion through the walls as well as her mom constantly yelling over the thumping on the walls. "Daddy let my momma go and leave her alone. I'm tired of seeing you fight mommy." "Move Cache'," Ron says. Your mom talks too much." "Let her go leave her alone," Cache' says crying. Dionne was trying to get away from Ron for she knew her daughter couldn't do anything to save her. When Ron finally let Dionne go she ran to the bathroom and closed and locked the door. "I told you I'm not going anywhere," Ron was yelling. Cache' balled up in the corner and cried. Her little legs were shaking. Ron walks over by her and try to grab her. She looked up at him with her beady eyes full of tears.

"Daddy please don't touch me I'm mad at you and I'm very scared. I just want my momma you hurt her." Ron just looked down at Cache' saying he's sorry. Just like Dionne, Cache' was used to the fake apologies Ron tried to give when he's done something wrong. "Daddy you always say sorry but you keep doing it over and over again." Ron kisses Cache' and sits on the bed.

"Please operator can you please send the police. I'm so scared my fiancé just beat me and I just want him to be escorted out my house because he won't leave on his own." "A unit is going to be there shortly. Where is he?" "He's in the room and I'm in the bathroom." "Ma'am you stay in there until the police arrive." "Yes ma'am." The doorbell rings. "Who is it?" Ron ask when he gets to the door. "The police open the door." The police Ron say to himself nervous. I know she didn't call them damn people. Dionne ran out the bathroom and opens the door for the police. "Are you alright ma'am?" "No sir, I just want him to get out my house. I want him to get his clothes and get out my house." "Come on sir and get your belongings and leave." "But sir, I pay all the bills." "Whose name is this house in?" The police ask. "My name," Dionne hurries and answers. "So that means you have to leave. Sir please do not harass her once you're gone. Ma'am if he bothers you again you will need to get a peace bond." "Alright officer I'm going to leave." Ron went in the room to pack his stuff. Cache' ran in the living room to hug her mom. "Are you alright?" "Yes, I'm alright baby." Ron walks in the living room with all his things. He walks over and kisses Cache' and walked out the door. He was out done when Dionne didn't do the usual. Running behind him screaming don't leave you promised you wouldn't leave. He thought to himself she must really mean it this time. The police tells Dionne to calm her baby down because she was very upset. "Thank you so much for coming out." "You welcome if you have anymore problems do not hesitate to give us a call." "Thanks." "Good night," the officers replied.

"Come on Cache' let's fix your brother a bottle for when he wakes up. I can't believe he slept through all this. I'm going to get your brother out his room and ya'll can sleep with me." "Mom can you turn a movie on please?" "I sure can." "Let me call Kimora and ask her to set me up to see a counselor I'm ready to start my new life." "Hey, Kimora, you think you can schedule me an appointment to see a counselor?" "When you want to go?" "It doesn't matter as soon as possible." "I'm going to get on that immediately Dionne." "Thanks sweetie call me and let me know when and what time I need to be there."

Ron pulls up to Donald's house. Donald was sitting on his porch. "My boy Ron. What's up you don't look to good. You look like you're stressed out." "I am bra." "What's the deal?" "You know about all that stuff that happened today by Shannon?" "Yeah right", Donald answers. "Well Dionne made me leave the house. When I got there I told her I wasn't leaving and then she called the police to escort me out." "What? She called the police? Damn man she wasn't playing." "No she wasn't." "You know Ron; women get tired of putting up with the same thing over and over again that's like men we wouldn't put with it. How many times you think you can hurt a woman before she gets fed up. You better go listen to R. Kelly's song he said it perfect, *"When a woman's fed up there is nothing you can do about it."* Man you have a beautiful daughter a handsome son and a girl that's down for you. What you were doing wasn't even worth the risk of losing your family." "You're right Donald." Soon as those hood rats find out that Dionne put you out they're going to be laughing at you and you know they gone be trying to get you over there cause they know all the things you did for Dionne." "Yeah, that's the truth." "Now you've lost your family over stupidity." "I'm fucked up right now man I feel lost. I don't know what I was thinking about." "You know it's fun until you get caught and your girl put her feet down." "If the shoe was on the other foot I wouldn't be able to handle it." "Then why you kept doing all that to her?" Donald asked. "D, I don't know being stupid not thinking she would ever leave. Everything I ever did she would be mad and hurt but she wouldn't leave. I guess I got to comfortable thinking she wasn't going anywhere. I really love Dionne with all my heart. I don't care about the rest of them hoes. Now I don't know what she's going to do. I wonder if she still wants me or if there is going to be someone else. I'm sorry for everything I did to her and what I put my kids through they didn't deserve this. I wanted to be out here head first and it back fired on my ass." "That's good you realize your faults now you need to get it together. That's the reason; I'm not dedicated to no one because I'm not ready to settle down," Donald expresses. "I don't want to hurt nobody and I don't want anybody to hurt me." "What have I done? I lost everythin a good family and a good home."

Dionne gets up the next morning; she brushes her teeth and washes her face. Dionne looks in the mirror and she felt like she just wanted to break down but as she was looking in the mirror she knew deep down inside she deserved better than Ron. Something was holding her together and she knew everything happens for a reason. "Good morning mommy," Cache' says. "Good morning my sweet angel. How are you doing this morning?" Dionne asks Cache'. "I'm doing well. Mommy I miss daddy." "I know you do sweetie he'll come visit you and your brother." "Cache' what you saw daddy do to me when you get older don't ever let a man do those things to you. You deserve to be happy all your life." "I won't mommy," Cache' responds. "Come on so you can get ready. I have to drop you off and mommy has an appointment to go to."

"Hey Brenda what's up?" "You Will I haven't heard from you in awhile." "I guess not if you haven't been calling my phone." "I have to call you in order to talk to you." "I didn't say that missy." "So what are you saying mister?" "I miss my pussy." "Your pussy, ha you're funny. It wasn't yours when you were having dinner with Akira." Will started laughing. "Your friends don't miss nothing right?" "They're not suppose to when it comes down to you." "I heard your girl and Ron separated huh?" "Boy word gets around quick especially to people like you that always have their ears open for information." "That's exactly right big booty. Now come give daddy some of that pussy." "Will, that's really what it's all about. You just want me for that." "Not really but that's all we have time to do when we're together." You know Will you're right that's all we did when we were together but now I feel different about the booty call relationship I want more for myself. I'm tired of giving myself to you for nothing." "Wait Brenda, what you was looking for a relationship?" "Are you serious Will?" "Yes, I am." "If I wanted a relationship with you in the beginning, I've changed my mind. I want a man not a dog." Will started laughing, "What you trying to be sarcastic?" "No I'm not but you can go ahead and stay with Akira and let her finish putting up with your dog ass. I am one woman that doesn't give a damn about how much money you have. It's all about respect you bastard," Brenda says as she hangs up the phone. "Hello, hello," Will says repeatedly. When he realized Brenda hung up her phone he looked at his phone and said out loud to himself that hoe is crazy. She better not call my phone again, Will say's upset.

CHAPTER XXVII

Dionne leaves her session feeling good and new about herself. She picked up her phone when she got in the car to call Kimora. "What's happening Kimora, this is Dionne." "Hey Dionne, I was waiting for you to call me how did your session go?" "It went well; I left out the building smiling." "Great; where you headed to now?" "That's the reason I'm calling you." "What's wrong Dionne?" Kimora asked anxious. "Calm down Kimora nothing is wrong; I'm on the way to this community center. The therapists recommend I go to share my story at Women's Night Out." "Really Kimora says screaming." "Yes girl and I need you to invite everybody Sasha, Ashley and the rest of the ladies. It would be nice for all of them to attend." "Yes Dionne I'll get on that right away." Thanks Kimora that's what I'm talking about. I appreciate it." Kimora hangs up the phone and immediately starts calling everybody.

"Can you please reach me her bottle Lily? This girl knows she has a big mouth." "She's a good baby compared to some babies Ashley." "If you say so Lily." "Have you heard from her deadbeat daddy Derrick?" "Yep he called like three days ago asking how is his baby. I damn near threw up. I told him jackass you haven't called me in four months and now all of sudden you want to know how she's doing. She's doing well without your sorry ass. He gone say damn it's like that Ashley? I asked him how the hell it's supposed to be you sperm donor." "Child I know he was shocked." "Was he Lily then he gone holler about she's his daughter too. I said oh now she's your daughter but when she was first born you didn't want to have nothing to do with her. You thought you were hurting me you see I wasn't calling your ass to ask you for nothing. I been holding us down like a mother that already knew she had a deadbeat dad for the father of her child. Your ass got a reality check and decided to call me to see what's up. I left him with this Lily. How are we doing? Good. Do we need you? Hell no. Do I want you to be apart of you daughter's life? That's on you but as you can see it makes me no difference." Lily starts jumping up and down. "You let his ass have it." "I sure did. I had him on that phone quiet. I said hello." He said I hear you sounding stupid. Then I asked him if that was all he needed? He said yeah I guess. I said you damn idiot and I hung up the phone." "That's good for his throwed off ass. Anyway are you coming with me to hear Dionne speak." "Yes indeed." "Well come on before we be late I don't want miss nothing."

CHAPTER XXVIII

"Hi Ms.Peters, I'm Dionne." "Hi Dionne I was expecting you. Let me show you around and you can bring your beautiful daughter to the nursery." When Dionne gets around the huge building to the nursery she tells Cache' to go in with the rest of the kids. "Their playing games and watching movies she'll be okay until you're finished." "Do good mom," Cache' says as she gave her mom a hug. A tear dropped from Dionne's eye she was speechless. "Thanks baby I will put forth my best. I don't know what I'd do without you."

Dionne walked off with Ms. Peters. "Dionne," Ms. Peters says, "you're up next." Dionne took a deep breath her knees got so weak she felt like she was about to pass out. Dionne closed her eyes and said a brief prayer. Lord I need you right now give me the words to say at this time. Dionne walks up to the mic, and begins to speak. The crowd of people stood up clapping. "Thank you, thank you. I really appreciate you coming out." She saw Ashley, Brenda, Lily, Kimora and even Nicollet there. My name is Dionne Jackson and I was a victim of domestic violence. I have been emotionally and physically abused. Almost everyday of the week I experienced having black eyes busted lips and bruises all over my body. I was cheated on with several different women. My abuser would stay out all hours of the night. None of his wrong doings were wrong in his eyes. If I asked him anything he would get agitated curse me out and then beat me. No matter how much I put out for him he still did what he wanted. My innocent children would scream to the top of their lungs. I loved him so much that I was scared to let him go. No matter how much my children were hurting from that bad situation I still stayed there. At the time I was so blind and foolishly in love that I didn't realize who and what really mattered. In the middle of Dionne's speech Ron walks in. Dionne and Ron made eye contact as he took a seat. I was so stressed out; I couldn't eat and I started losing weight. I was throwing up and crying out the blue. This man disgraced me he dishonored me and he disrespected me so much he made me think I was the worst person on earth. He brought me down to my lowest point. He made me think I wasn't worth nothing to the point I started believing that I really wasn't worth nothing. I guess that's why I stayed so long. I didn't even like myself anymore. My self esteem was so low I even contemplated suicide. If it wasn't for my children I don't know I just might have tried. The last time he beat me I felt like I was going to die. I was so scared. When I got away from him I called the police for help. I fell on my knees and begged God to deliver me from it all. Dionne starts to cry. I cried out to him non-stop asking him to give me the strength to love myself more than man. I wanted to love God more than anything. After that I knew no weapon formed against me was going to prosper. I knew he was making my enemy my footstool. God said I am the head and not the tail. He told me the battle was not mine it is his. After I had a talk with Jesus I made up my mind to let go and let God. I became stronger and stronger day by day and now I am able to share my story with you all. I can now face my challenges. I pray that my words have encouraged you to want better and to know that whatever you are going through man or woman God will see you through it. Dionne was so joyous that she began to cry. She grabbed a tissue and tried to keep her composure. Dionne looked at Ron and she was surprised to see tears coming out of Ron's eyes. Her speech seemed as though it had an impact on everyone in the room. The women were shouting and crying and hugging each other. Dionne continues on, "I hope I've touched someone's spirit here today. We as women do not have to belittle ourselves for no man. Love God first then yourself. Our children don't deserve to go through so many negative changes in there innocent lives. So I challenge you women and men today to get out of unhealthy relationships. It's just not worth it you deserve more and your worth more. No matter how much you try to change a man or woman it want work unless their ready to change. All you can do is pray for them. So stand up trust in God and love yourself no matter what. Thank you for coming out," Dionne says before she steps down off the stage. Women and men were coming up hugging Dionne telling her thank you for being brave to come out and tell her story to other people. Some said she really would make a difference in their relationship. One lady told Dionne her daughter died in an abusive relationship. She says her daughter's husband stabbed her daughter in the back of the head and he left her there to die. I am so sorry to hear that. Nicolett walks up to Dionne telling her, I really respeat you coming out and speaking on that situation because your not the only one he did that to." "I thank you for coming out Nicolett.

Ron walks up to Dionne. "How are you?" Ron asks. "I'm great Ronald and you?" "I'm not doing to good since our break up." "Really Ronald?" "Yes I want to tell you, you did a wonderful job up there." "Thanks Ronald that just shows you everything I went through with you only made me a stronger woman." Ron couldn't believe what he was hearing. "Dionne I am so sorry. If I could take it all back I would be a better person." Dionne hugged Ron and whispered in his ear, "It's too late baby." Then she looked him in his eyes and told him, "I won't stop praying for you. You will one day make a good husband to someone. You are welcome to come see your children at anytime just make sure you call before you come." Dionne walked off. "Dionne," Ron called. Dionne turned around. "You are a good woman and you will make a beautiful wife." It hurted Ron to his heart to acknowledge that. Dionne smiled at Ron and tells him "Thanks and God bless."

CHAPTER XXIX

Dionne got Cache' and they went to the café. Dionne was reading the paper when a guy walked up to her. "How's your day beautiful?" Not even looking up Dionne replied. "Good, thank you." "I don't mean to bother you but if you don't mind me asking are you married?" "Actually I'm not," Dionne says looking up at the man. I just got out of a relationship." "I would like to leave you my number and hope you think about calling me one day when you're not busy. The guy handed Dionne his card. 'I think I will just to that." Enjoy the rest of your day and you too," he said to Cache'. Dionne and Cache' both smiled as the man walked off. Dionne looked at the card and it read Entrepreneur: Landen Tshiteya.

Ron was driving in his car listening to his radio. When a woman's fed up by R. Kelly came on Ron started thinking about the times he and Dionne spent together and how he and his children got along so good. Ron's phone rings. He picks it up, what the hell does she want as he read Shannon's name across the screen. "What?" He said when he answers. "Why are you answering your phone so harsh? You forgot I'm your baby momma." "That's why I'm not with my family right not because of you and your daughter. You should've had an abortion when I told you to." "It's our daughter just in case you forgot and I wasn't killing my baby because you had a family." "You know what Shannon I didn't want the baby and you knew that. Damn you," Ron hung up the phone and blasts his music as he drove off with the wind.